Making a Pilgrimage

Making a Pilgrimage

SALLY WELCH

LION

A Lion Book
an imprint of
Lion Hudson plc
Wilkinson House, Jordan Hill Road,
Oxford OX2 8DR, England
www.lionhudson.com

ISBN 978 0 7459 5356 4 (UK)
ISBN 978 0 8254 7869 7 (US)

Distributed by:
UK: Marston Book Services Ltd, PO Box 269, Abingdon,
Oxon, OX14 4YN
USA: Trafalgar Square Publishing, 814 N. Franklin Street,
Chicago, IL 60610
USA: Christian Market: Kregel Publications, PO Box 2607,
Grand Rapids, MI 49501

First edition 2009
10 9 8 7 6 5 4 3 2 1 0

Acknowledgments
Every effort has been made to trace and acknowledge copyright holders of all the
quotations included. We apologize for any errors or omissions that may remain,
and would ask those concerned to contact the publishers, who will ensure that
full acknowledgment is made in the future.
p 23 U2, 'Walk On', Island Records, New York; p 30 Dag Hammerskjöld, taken
from *To Speak for the World: Speeches and Statements by Dag Hammerskjöld*,
(ed. K. Falkman), Stockholm, Atlantis; pp 120 & 123 Excerpts from "Little
Gidding" in *The Four Quartets*, copyright 1942 by T. S. Eliot and renewed 1970
by Esme Valerie Eliot, reprinted by permission of Houghton Mifflin Harcourt
Publishing Company and Faber & Faber Ltd.
Scripture quotations are from the Contemporary English Version published
by The Bible Societies/HarperCollins Publishers copyright © 1991, 1992, 1995
American Bible Society.

This book has been printed on paper independently certified as having been
produced from sustainable forests.

A catalogue record for this book is available
from the British Library

Typeset in Warnock Pro 10/14.5
Printed and bound in Malta

To Jeremy, Jessie, Si, Ellie and Binka,
with love

Contents

Acknowledgments

Grateful thanks to John and Pat Barker, Nick and Margaret Yates, Tony Wales and Kate Kirkpatrick

Introduction

It is good to have an end to journey towards, but it is the journey that matters in the end.
Ursula K. Le Guin

Pilgrimage is a meaningful journey to a sacred place. A pilgrimage can be made in the context of an established faith such as Christianity, to a world-famous site such as Santiago de Compostela, or it can be made for other reasons. The essence of pilgrimage is a journey made in a spirit of searching, with an openness to what the journey can teach.

This book is a guide to pilgrimage:

✳ It is a history book – it will help you to put your journey in the context of the journeys of others.

✳ It is an instruction book – it won't tell you what to pack for your journey, but it will help you to work out what to leave behind.

✳ It is a gazetteer – it will help you to make sense of the sites you walk past and use them for your own reflections.

✳ It is a map – although it won't tell you where to go, it will tell you how to get there.

✳ It is a manual – it will show you how you can learn and grow through your experiences on pilgrimage.

✳ It is a companion – keep it by your side as you journey, interact with it, use it to record your experiences and reflections and add them to those of this book.

How to Use This Book

This book doesn't differentiate between methods of travel: whether you undertake your pilgrimage by car or bus, by bike, or, seeking to emulate the first pilgrims, by doing the entire journey on foot, the topics in this book will be useful to you, and the reflections can be adapted to fit your own situation and circumstances. Little mention is made of specific pilgrim routes or the length of your journey – whether you are planning a three-month trip to Santiago de Compostela, or a day's journey to a local sacred site, the experience of pilgrimage can be a spiritual and fruitful one. Even if you are unable to make a physical journey of pilgrimage, you can follow the route of your own 'armchair' pilgrimage, using the notes and reflections in this book.

Each chapter follows the same format, beginning with a quotation on the theme of the chapter, followed by a story of the author's pilgrim experience. These stories are for your reflection, to ask whether your reaction to the experience would have been similar, or whether you would have approached things differently. The next section puts the topic in historical context, looking at the way a pilgrim in times gone by might have experienced similar events, followed by a discussion of how you can learn from this experience yourself.

Each chapter ends with a reflection designed for you to use on your journey. They use no special equipment (not even candles!). All you need is space, time and the occasional prop that you will easily find in your surroundings.

You don't have to read this book from cover to cover. You can, of course, do so, but you can also dip into the book, choosing sections that are relevant to your journey, and perhaps never using some if they do not appeal.

A Brief Outline of Pilgrimage

From earliest times, people have gone on pilgrimage. Evidence has been uncovered of aboriginal peoples making sacred journeys in prehistoric times. Centuries later, the pagan shrine of Apollo at Delphi was visited by the Ancient Greeks. For the Jewish people, life as a sacred journey was a recurring theme: 'the word GO is seared into the very flesh of Israel', as Richard Giles expresses it in *Re-pitching the Tent* – and this impetus to pilgrimage carried over into Christian civilization. Eager to see and touch the places where Jesus was physically present, pilgrims from as early as the fourth century journeyed to Jerusalem. St Helena, mother of Constantine, first journeyed to Jerusalem in AD 326, returning with many of the earliest relics, and from AD 385 we have the first pilgrim's guidebook, *Itinerarium Egeriae* (*Travels of Egeria*). Journeying to visit the sites of the Christian story expanded as the veneration of saints developed, and by the beginning of the Middle Ages, pilgrimage was a fundamental part of European Christian life. A relatively stable Europe meant that pilgrim routes could be developed that criss-crossed much of the continent, leading even as far as Jerusalem. The rise in the popularity of pilgrimage from the eleventh century to its peak in the fifteenth century charts a 'progression from private austerity to popular enthusiasm', according to historian Jonathan Sumption. However, by the late fifteenth century, it had become largely debased – an excuse for travelling in large and often raucous companies, seeking to get away from the monotony of medieval life.

As the resurgence of local conflicts in areas of Spain and France at the end of the fifteenth century coincided with the wars in Jerusalem, pilgrimage turned into crusading, and the routes became unsafe. The end of pilgrimage came quite suddenly, stricken as it was by the renewal of hostilities in Europe and the Far East, which made travel a life-threatening activity, and also by the growing strength of the theological argument put forward by Gregory of Nyssa – that God was not only present in certain places but could be sought and found anywhere. The Reformation in Europe in the sixteenth century brought with it the idea that pilgrimage was in fact a spiritually unnecessary thing. Martin Luther, one of the most famous figures of the Reformation, argued strongly that pilgrimage merely offered more opportunities to break God's commandments. It was better, he said, to spend one's energies looking after friends and neighbours at home. English clergymen were instructed to preach against pilgrimage to relics, and with the destruction of many shrines and holy places under the order of Henry VIII in the 1540s, pilgrimage sites themselves became rarer.

The Thirty Years War in Europe rendered pilgrimage still less attractive. The end of the war in 1648 coincided with the advent of Puritanism and the rule of Oliver Cromwell and his parliament, to whom the concept of pilgrimage was anathema. The only spiritual journey contemplated was one of the mind; indeed this period saw the most famous allegorical pilgrimage of all: John Bunyan's *Pilgrim's Progress*, in which Christian, burdened with sin, makes the difficult and dangerous journey from the 'City of Destruction' (this world) to the 'Celestial City' (heaven).

The Enlightenment of the late seventeenth century brought with it the concept of the Grand Tour. This was typically a coming-of-age journey made by young men who brought back souvenirs, sometimes in the form of relics, from spiritual and artistic shrines. Rome and Jerusalem featured prominently on these journeys. But travel was still too expensive and dangerous for most people, and the advent of the French Revolution in 1789 brought this temporary resurgence to a close.

The end of the Napoleonic Wars in 1815 meant Europe was once again safe for travellers, and pilgrimage enjoyed another revival. This may in part have been as a reaction to the increased industrialization and mechanization in several European countries. A sense of displacement caused by mass migration into new towns and cities may have led people to seek out the community of the road journey. A more matter-of-fact and scientific approach to life also seems to have led many to wish to see for themselves the geographic locations on which the story of their Christian faith was based.

Two World Wars and increased secularization led to pilgrimage once again declining in popularity, but recently, amid the resurgence of interest in exploring different types of spirituality, it has enjoyed a significant revival. The number of pilgrims travelling to Santiago de Compostela in Spain, for example, increased from a mere 2,491 in 1984 to 100,377 in 2006, and continues to rise. Today pilgrimage is more popular than ever. Although the reasons for undertaking a pilgrimage appear to be different from those of the original medieval pilgrim, these sacred journeys give people space to step aside from the circumstances of their lives in order to reflect upon them. Challenging and demanding both physically and mentally, pilgrimage can be a life-changing adventure.

Of course, reasons for pilgrimage still encompass the traditional ones of healing – particularly with regards to places such as Lourdes – and of penance (detailed in the next chapter). However, today there is far more emphasis on spiritual searching by the individual – looking for a spiritual certainty that perhaps was a given for the medieval pilgrim. Books on spirituality have been written with pilgrimage – both spiritual and physical – as the theme, and there is recognition of the value of the metaphor of pilgrimage for one's journey through life.

Pilgrims walk to change themselves; they walk to find meaning. Previously held to be the place where meaning was found, a shrine is now often merely the indicator of the end of the journey – it is the journey itself that is the transformative experience. Pilgrimage is about 'encouraging those who initially may be attracted by the lure of the holy place and the romantic destination to think about their own lives and their inner journey', as Ian Bradley writes in *Colonies of Heaven*. Once on the route, the travellers find themselves making a pilgrimage, both through their own expectations and through the culture around them. Their identity is, according to Bradley, 'socially conferred as well as personally created', and intrinsic to the nature of the modern pilgrimage is the sense of community that is built up by pilgrims on the journey.

Nor is this sense of community limited to those in whose company the pilgrim is currently journeying. The modern pilgrim is reminded at every turn in the road, by shrines, by signs, by centuries-old footpaths, that the road they are treading now has been walked by thousands of people over hundreds of years. This, in turn, has an effect on how they see their journey and their own expectations of it. The whole of life is seen as a journey, with no particular earthly destination apparent or necessary.

Leaving

Why Journey?

Success is not a place at which one arrives but rather the spirit with which one undertakes and continues the journey.

Alex Noble

We were having one of those intense conversations that can take place between strangers who have been thrown together by circumstance. Sitting round a rough wooden table, removed from the self-imposed limitations of status, discretion and self-protection, we were discussing the original reasons that lay behind our decision to make this particular pilgrimage. 'I had been drawn to pilgrimage through its power as a tool for meditation and prayer,' I said. The man opposite roared with laughter – his motive had been adventure and the challenge of travelling alone carrying all that was necessary for survival on his back. My neighbour, a neat, compactly built Belgian in his early middle age, hesitated a bit, as if unsure how to articulate his feelings. 'I had a business,' he said. 'It was not a big one, but it was moderately successful. I had a wife and two sons, a nice house, a quiet life. But then the business started to go wrong. I worked harder and harder to try to put it right. My wife grew tired of waiting for me to come home late each night, still preoccupied with my work problems. She left with my children. The business collapsed. I lost the house. I have nothing left in my life now. I am walking to try to make sense of it all, and to try to find the courage to start again.'

It may be true that the earliest of pilgrims travelled with a single purpose, or at least a small number of straightforward reasons. What is certain, though, is that the desire to go on a sacred journey to show love for a saint and pray for forgiveness and healing, as Thomas Aquinas wrote about in the late thirteenth century, rapidly became overlaid with many others. The unifying factor among all pilgrims, regardless of their motivation, was that they were on a journey of purpose.

At the core of the concept of pilgrimage was the belief that there were certain places that were special to God, where the gap between heaven and earth was thinner than in ordinary places and where, consequently, there was greater spiritual power. The most obvious of these places were those where Jesus had lived, stayed, preached and died, and as Jonathan Sumption wrote, 'the most celebrated tomb visited by pilgrims in the Middle Ages was empty'. Yet other places too were held to be of great importance, if not quite as significant as Jerusalem. Rome, with its connection to St Peter and

Santiago, home of the body of St James, made up the 'big three' pilgrimage destinations alongside Jerusalem, above hundreds of lower-ranking sites. By travelling to places where saints had lived or performed miracles, pilgrims sought their closeness and favour. It was also felt that places made holy by people or events brought one closer to eternity. The shrine served as a bridge between this world and the next, between the reality of earth and the possibility of heaven, and by visiting these sacred places, one's personal salvation might be made more certain.

Many of these shrines were made famous by the miracles that had been witnessed there, often miracles of healing; a desire for an end to suffering was a powerful reason for undertaking a pilgrimage. In medieval times, ill health was prevalent, doctors were few and poorly equipped, diet was bad and sanitary conditions were worse, to such an extent that people rarely felt completely well. Any chance to alleviate unpleasant and painful symptoms would be seized upon eagerly. Equally, though, a pilgrimage could be undertaken in a spirit of thanksgiving: in gratitude for an unexpected healing or a reprieve from danger.

In many cases, however, the sickness was not physical but mental or spiritual. While death from disease or injury was an ever-present threat, fear of judgment in an afterlife played a major part in people's relationship with religion. Penitential pilgrimages were common as people tried to assuage God's possible anger at their wrongdoings by undertaking difficult and dangerous tasks. By the eleventh century this concept had become formalized into the notion that the automatic remission of sins could be obtained by an official visit to a particular shrine, and there was even a ranking system whereby more serious sins entailed longer pilgrimages as penance, Jerusalem being reserved for only the most formidable of crimes. This idea even became incorporated into the justice system in England the twelfth and thirteenth centuries enforced pilgrimage was an effective punishment for many crimes. On the other hand, pilgrims *en route* were immune from any criminal or civil suits brought against them, a law which led to some people becoming lifelong pilgrims!

In contrast, there was also the desire to escape from the evils of society. To renounce the burden of civilization and journey unencumbered in search of spiritual enlightenment was a powerful motivating factor behind many pilgrimages. Medieval life was very restrictive and quite repetitive: the opportunity to travel was severely limited, and any chances, however risky, were often enthusiastically seized upon. As pilgrimage routes became better defined and the infrastructure of guesthouses more sophisticated, the appeal of pilgrimage grew. Although it would be an exaggeration to say that by the fifteenth century the adventure of pilgrimage had displaced other, more spiritual motives, it was certainly an increasingly prevalent reason.

As the popularity of pilgrimage lessened, the

spirituality of the journey once again came to the forefront. In the novel *Tancred*, Benjamin Disraeli writes of the protagonist's desire to visit those places where Jesus lived in order to answer some deep questions: 'What is duty and what is faith? What ought I to do and what ought I believe?'

Seeking spiritual adventure remains a prominent motive for pilgrimages to this day. Many studies have been undertaken on the reasons people decide to embark on what can still be an arduous, lonely and time-consuming trip, depending on the chosen mode of transport. Though there seem to be as many motives as there are pilgrims, a broad consensus does emerge. Just as in medieval times, many people seek healing through pilgrimage. It might be a straightforward search for physical healing, such as that which impels many of the pilgrims who travel to Lourdes each year, or more complicated spiritual and psychological healing, which is also sought and often found amid the journeying and arrival. Others travel to celebrate relationships – couples may journey to a site on their anniversary – or to put the strength of a new relationship to the test through the gauntlet of difficult circumstances. A desire to escape everyday life, with its restrictions and limitations, can be very powerful. With this desire, there may also be a wish to seek the time and space in which to find meaning and personal transformation. Those whose lives appear to have reached a dead end, or whose life circumstances have taken an unexpected turn, travel to find space and possible resolution of the past and resolve for the future.

Pilgrimage can be undertaken in fulfilment of a promise, as a way of prayer or as a journey to spiritual wholeness. It can be a cultural excursion or a historical tour, as the buildings along the path reflect different stages in a country's history. The path itself forms the basis for a community, stretching back through time and across the globe. The most important thing for the contemporary pilgrim, however, is to actually decide to journey, and once the decision has been made, to act upon it.

Reflection

What is your reason for going on pilgrimage?
Reflect honestly on what it is that is making you
undertake this journey. Are your reasons powerful
enough to keep you going through the difficult
parts? List five reasons on a piece of paper. Then
burn the list – on the journey you are about to
undertake, you need to be open to all possible ways
of transformation. Do not limit yourself to what
you think you will gain or learn. Instead, let the
experience teach in its own way.

What to Take, What to Leave Behind

**And love is not the easy thing
The only baggage you can bring
And love is not the easy thing…
The only baggage you can bring
Is all that you can't leave behind**
U2, 'Walk On'

Some years ago, I had the privilege of accompanying a regiment of British soldiers on an exercise in Scotland. Since what they could take was severely limited, the soldiers had become very skilled at working out what was necessary and what was superfluous. Equipment was in three parts. In a large bergen was everything needed for the month-long exercise. A smaller pack held the items necessary for that particular day or piece of work. Finally, a soldier's webbing contained only those things that were essential for basic survival – ammunition, emergency rations, etc. However, I was interested to note that in addition to the necessities, every soldier carried with them something that made life on exercise slightly more bearable. Highly personal objects, these had been selected over the years as the things that helped keep morale up during the difficult times. They ranged from a bottle of Tabasco sauce or Earl Grey tea bags to an embroidery kit – each object as individual as those who took them.

It was desirable to travel as lightly as possible, emulating Jesus' first followers, who were sent out to tell his story with no money or equipment, reliant upon the kindness of those they met. From early times, however, pilgrims had a clearly defined 'uniform' that distinguished them from merchants and other travellers. Most important of all was a letter of commendation from the pilgrim's overlord giving permission to undertake the journey. This entitled them to the privileges of a pilgrim and made them eligible for the hospitality on which their journey relied, including food and lodgings. By 1388 it was an arrestable offence for a pilgrim to travel without these documents, or *testimoniales*. A pilgrim would wear the special clothing of a tunic or *sclavein* and a cloak. Those travelling to Jerusalem would bear a red cross on the shoulder of the cloak. The pilgrim would carry a staff, partly for protection against dogs and other attackers, and also as a symbol of the role of a pilgrim, along with a bag or scrip, usually with a strap going across the body, which contained the all-important letter of safe conduct, food, water and a few other items for the journey. These clothes and equipment became very dear to those who wore them – the body of a pilgrim found under the main tower in Worcester Cathedral had been buried in his boots, with his staff and bag by his side, as well as scallop shells, a symbol of the pilgrimage to Santiago de Compostela.

The same injunction to take as little as possible with you for the journey holds true to this day, if for no other reason than because any journey is made easier with less luggage to encumber it! The purpose of this book is not to give advice over exactly what to pack, but a few guidelines might come in handy. It is a commonly held belief that to carry more than ten per cent of one's body weight in a backpack is to invite fatigue, backache and quite a lot of misery, unless one is of the super-fit variety of pilgrim. Practice journeys, ideally with an overnight stay, are invaluable for helping decide which things can be left behind and which would ruin your trip by their absence. Do try, however, to fit in a journal in which to record your thoughts, as well as extras such as blister plasters to give away to others who might need them, and at least one luxury to make your journey easier.

All items for packing pale in significance beside the attitude that you take with you on the journey. It is vital to leave behind all fixed expectations, all narrowness of heart and mind, all assumptions about people and places. Take with you instead an attitude of expectancy, of hopefulness, of willingness to be changed and transformed. Be determined to seize all new experiences and ideas, to seek the new and the unfamiliar, and to reassess your role and purpose in life.

Reflection

Look at the things you want to take along on your journey. See them as reflections of the spiritual things you are taking. Some of these spiritual objects are like bricks – totally unnecessary, serving only to make the pack burdensome. Are you taking with you a materialist anxiety, a concern that what you

*have might not be enough, or might reflect badly
on you? Are you taking with you regrets, whether
from childhood or from last week? Are you carrying
feelings that block an attitude of thanksgiving and
hopefulness? Determine to take with you only the
important things: your beliefs, your love for those
with whom you share your life, a generous spirit and
an open heart.*

Reflection

*On separate pieces of paper, write down the attitudes
and feelings you wish to leave behind on your
journey. They can be big things like 'prejudice', 'fear',
'anxiety', or smaller irritations such as 'not the food
I am used to'. Add to them in the days before your
departure. Place these under a large stone, or a pile
of stones, near the entrance to your dwelling. Let
them be the last thing you see before you leave.*

Rituals for Departure

**Farewell! a word that must be, and hath been,
A sound which makes us linger; yet–farewell!**
Childe Harold's Pilgrimage Stanza, 1670

Not without some misgivings, my husband had allowed me to tack
on an extra week to our holiday so that I could walk on my own
part of the Route St Jacques, one of the pilgrim paths that runs

through France, before picking up the Camino de Santiago de Compostela at the Spanish border. I was being driven to a starting point just south of Bourges, inaccessible by public transport, so the family clambered into the car to see me off. Halfway along a small country road where the path led off along a hedgerow, we stopped. I got out, shouldered my backpack and set off, walking rather too fast for comfort, wanting to impress everyone with how fit and energetic I was. The family car drove off and I was alone. As I walked along I realized I felt a sense of incompleteness, of something not done – it took me the whole of one field edge before I realized that I had not set off properly. So intent had I been on issuing the usual last-minute instructions, on hugging everyone and then striding away quickly before we all changed our minds, that I had not taken time to get into the correct frame of mind for beginning such a journey. Reluctantly, I retraced my steps to where I had begun and spent some time at my starting point clearing my mind, and preparing myself mentally for the journey. Then, once again, I shouldered my backpack and set off. Now I was ready.

Farewells have always been deeply significant. Aware that the journey that was about to be undertaken was one from which the pilgrim might not return, the farewell rituals of historic pilgrims grew in complexity until the entire community was involved. The local church might play a part: before a medieval pilgrim left, he would seek the church's blessing on his journey. After confessing his sins, a special mass might be said to commend the pilgrim to God and to service as a pilgrim. Each item of his clothing would be sprinkled with holy water and blessed, and then the pilgrim would be sent on his way. Often he would be escorted to the city gates or just outside the town by members of the village or tradesman's guild, sometimes with the additional benefit of a collection made for him by his friends and fellow workers. As travel became safer, this farewell party diminished merely to family and close friends, or even, in the case of latter-day pilgrim Hilaire Belloc in 1902, to a simple setting out one morning.

When pilgrim groups set out today, there is often opportunity for a ritualized farewell. In addition to this, at various points along the way, churches might hold special pilgrims' masses, during which the pilgrims will be prayed for and blessed. If journeying alone, however, it is important to make sure that there is a sense of occasion attached to the departure from home, so that one's focus may be fully directed upon the journey.

Reflection

If possible, invite friends and family to a farewell gathering some days before you set off. Share with them your hopes and expectations for the journey, and ask them to hold you in their hearts as you travel.

Write the names of everybody you hold dear on a piece of paper. Be prepared for this to take some time and for there to be a lot of names! When this is done, place it somewhere safe as a symbol of your hope for their safety and continued well-being while you are away.

As you leave, take with you a transitional object – something that means 'home' to you. It may be a photograph, the mug you drink your tea from or a particular type of food. When you get to the doorway of your home, place the object there and turn your face toward the future.

On the Journey

Journeying with Integrity

A task becomes a duty from the moment you suspect it to be an essential part of that integrity which alone entitles a man to assume responsibility.

Dag Hammarskjöld, from *Markings*

'Ah, pilgrimage,' said the man sitting next to me at a conference. 'My daughter spent three weeks walking along the pilgrimage way to Santiago de Compostela. She said it was marvellous and came back so enthusiastic that my wife and her friend decided they wanted to walk it too. The friend's husband and I thought we would go too. We wouldn't do any walking, but we would take the car to provide backup and drive around seeing the sights and eating out while they walked, and then all meet up in the evenings.' The man paused and laughed. 'Do you know, I don't think the women walked more than 10 km in total. The temptation to get a lift in the car was just too much, you see!'

John O'Gaunt, son of King Edward III and father of Henry IV, was one of the richest and most powerful men in fourteenth-century England. In 1386 he too chose to undertake a pilgrimage, but unlike other rich and powerful men, his reasons were not at all spiritual or even adventurous. The journey to which he gave the title 'pilgrimage' would perhaps be better described as a tactical procession to validate his claim, through his wife's family, to be the King of Castile and Leon. Far from seeking absolution from his sins, when arriving at the sacred site of Santiago de Compostela he deposed the Archbishop and put his own man in place, before continuing his journey, unrepentant. John O'Gaunt did not travel alone or on foot, but with a huge and magnificent entourage and as many comforts as the age afforded. Throughout history, pilgrims have argued about the level of hardship required to prove one's devoutness of purpose, balancing the need for safety and enough funds for emergencies with the desire to rid oneself of unnecessary luxuries.

Today, with so many reasons for undertaking pilgrimage, it is not so necessary to prove one's seriousness of purpose by deliberately taking on hardships. As in most other human occupations, an element of competitiveness always creeps in: those who are making a pilgrimage on foot may pride themselves on how many kilometres they can walk each day, the prize going to the one who has walked furthest, fastest, longest; all walkers look down on those who are cycling;

those who have backup in the form of companions travelling by car are scorned by both walkers and cyclists, and all three groups dismiss those who make their journey by coach as not worthy of the name of pilgrim. These distinctions do not matter – what is important is that you select the method of travel that is right for you, and follow it, even if that method is occasionally difficult or uncongenial.

Each mode of transport carries with it its own obligations. The cyclist must give way to the walker when it comes to accommodation – the cyclist can, after all, more easily travel further in search of somewhere else to stay. The car driver can offer help to both walker and cyclist, without compromising the integrity of their journeys. Fresh water, extra supplies and repair materials can all be offered as part of the service pilgrims are obliged to offer their fellow travellers. The walker too is under an obligation to complete the journey without seeking too much assistance in the way of lifts or bus rides, unless circumstances dictate otherwise. The occasional lift, especially on a hot day with a lot of ground to cover, can be one of the blessings that is most vividly remembered when the journey is finally complete.

Finding Your Way

Don't believe what your eyes are telling you. All they show is limitation. Look with your understanding, find out what you already know, and you'll see the way to fly.

Richard Bach, from *Jonathan Livingston Seagull*

The guidebook I was using was all in French, and although excellent and wonderful in its thoroughness, there were some aspects of the path description that were perhaps a little too clear. I had not known before I started, for example, exactly how many words there were for different types of path and their construction material – it seemed to me almost as exhaustive a vocabulary as that of the Inuit and their words for snow. We came to a particularly challenging description, where the walker was invited to follow no fewer than four different types of path in quick succession, each one with a turning to the left or right, just to confuse matters. I stumbled along, ignoring the landscape, focusing on what our next movements should be. Suddenly my companion announced: 'The path goes over there, through the trees.' 'How on earth did you work that out?' I asked, surprised and a little annoyed. 'Simple,' he said, and pointed to the signs nailed onto the trees, each bearing the distinctive yellow shell showing which direction to take.

From the seventh century guidebooks to the major pilgrim routes were available, and as early as the ninth century phrasebooks were being used by travellers in Germany to demand hospitality, containing simple phrases like 'I want a drink.' By the twelfth century route books such as *Guide to Pilgrims to Santiago* were being carried by wealthier pilgrims in their bags. This book in particular contained both historical and factual information, with information on local towns, useful Basque words and a detailed route description. It also listed the possible dangers and difficulties the hapless traveller could experience, as well as places where there was a shortage of food and supplies. The famous *Liber Sancti Jacobi*, also from the twelfth century, was a collection of five books designed to help the pilgrim on his journey. The collection contained songs and hymns, stories of the miracles of St James, instructions for behaviour and dress of pilgrims as well as a guide to the routes and shrines along the way. As the routes became better organized, these route guides were superseded by books of indulgences, such as *The Pilgrimages and Pardons of Acre*, written in 1280. In these books, pilgrimage sites were listed according to how much a pilgrim's time in purgatory would be reduced should he visit the site and pray there. Poorer pilgrims, however, could not afford these guides, and could not have read them anyway. They relied on word of mouth, help from those living along the route, and, of course, the path itself spread out in front of them, marked by the feet of those who had gone before.

There will always be times when route-finding is

challenging, when the signs do not match the map, which does not match the guide. This must be taken as part of the gift of the journey. Being willing to accept the dangers of getting lost is part of the relationship that you will build up with the pilgrim way. So, too, is the ability to step off the path for a while, to take time to explore a town or village that is interesting or unusual. Timetables, however well-intentioned, should not be written in stone, lest the incidental gifts that the path offers you in the form of buildings, landscape and people be lost and your experience poorer.

Reflection
Step off the path for a moment and take time to think about your own path through life. Has it been straightforward? Has everything gone as you planned it should? Have the unexpected turnings in your life improved it or made it worse? How can this be changed? Draw a picture of your life as if it were a map – include swamps, mountains with wonderful views or dangerous precipices, green valleys or bleak wildernesses. Reflect on the picture this makes. Is there any way you could or should be making changes in direction?

Journaling

(Lord's day). Up and to church, where Mr Mills, [preached] a good sermon, and so home and had a good dinner with my wife, with which I was pleased to see it neatly done, and this troubled me to think of parting with Jane, that is come to be a very good cook.

Samuel Pepys, from *The Diary of Samuel Pepys*

In the evenings, after the showering and the sock-washing, but before the meal, it's 'journal time' in the pilgrim hostels. A multitude of notebooks emerge, large and small, expensive leather-bound journals and cheap ring-bound notebooks. Pens and pencils scrawl across the page amid an intense silence as the pilgrims commit their thoughts and feelings, their impressions of the day and its events, to their journals. Mostly these entries are written rapidly, without much reflection – the aim is merely to capture on paper what has happened before its imprint on the memory is overwritten by the next day's experiences and encounters. The reflection will come later, during a rest day on the journey or even after the pilgrim has returned home. Rereading the entries after the journey has ended brings a flood of memory and the opportunity to reflect on all that has happened and integrate the experience into daily life.

From the earliest days of travelling, those who travelled and could write would often feel drawn to write about their experiences, and much of the information we have on medieval pilgrimages comes from them. Some accounts, such as *The Travels of Sir John Mandeville*, are combinations of myth and reality, while others, by such travellers as William Wey, Bertrandon de la Brocquière and Margery Kempe, who were writing in the thirteenth and fourteenth centuries, portray their experiences on the road more factually.

This practice continued though the centuries, and if you look up 'journal' on the internet you are almost completely overrun with entries. Individuals' personal journals jostle for attention with online journal-writing workshops, advertisements for journaling courses, purpose-made journals complete with thoughts in case you have none of your own, endless instruction and advice on journal-writing itself, as well as notes on the experiences of others! Beginning to journal is more straightforward than these websites can lead you to believe, however, and can be very useful as a way not just of capturing moments and events, but of helping you to reflect on them later.

The first and most important thing to grasp is that there is no one right way to use a journal to deepen your spiritual life. Try experimenting with many different ways of journaling your experiences and thoughts until you find one that is comfortable. A different way may work better in a few months, so keep experimenting. Nevertheless, there are a few general guidelines that you may find helpful.

Firstly, do not confuse a journal with a diary. It is not necessary to record daily details in your journal – use it more as a travel record of your spiritual journey. A journal can take many different forms. It can be written as letters to a person or being. It can be poetry. It can be a list of thoughts, meditations on a subject or it can focus on good moments of the day – counting your blessings – and contain reflections on people encountered on the journey.

Many people find that 'thinking things through on paper' allows many new ideas, insights and attitudes to develop that otherwise might only have emerged with the help of a counsellor or spiritual director. Some maintain a regular journal, often over many years; others will keep a journal only during a retreat or at a time of stress or decision-making.

To write a journal might not seem like a spiritual activity, but it may help you to ask the underlying questions 'Where is the meaning in all this?' or 'Where does it seem that I should be going in all this?' It can be a way of 'seeing' our feelings. You can buy purpose-made journals – many high-street booksellers stock very attractive journals in all sorts of sizes and designs. Do buy one that you find attractive, and ideally a fairly small one, since it will have to fit in your backpack. Whatever it is like, though, it must be a pleasure to write in and easy to use.

Set aside a regular time for writing. Many pilgrims like to write as their first rest activity on arriving at a hostel; others prefer to write in the morning. The real benefits of journaling come from doing it regularly. You are more likely to write if you have a set time planned, and if you persist it will become a habit that you look forward to each day. I used to journal every night when I sat beside my babies while they settled. Now that they are older, I find first thing in the morning an easier time. Don't worry about how much you write each day: some days you will want to write a lot, other days just a few notes will be enough. You might be someone for whom writing does not come easily, in which case a few lines will do, or a sketch that reminds you of the day and how you felt about it.

Having said that, one comment I often hear is 'I start a journal, write every day for a few weeks and then stop. I can't seem to keep it going.' The most important thing here is to remember that it is okay to miss a day – this does not mean that the whole journaling exercise is not going to work for you. Just pick up your pen again the next day. Similarly, don't worry about spelling or grammar and don't feel you need to reread what you have written and edit it. Unless you are writing with the specific intention of publishing your journal, nobody but you is ever going to read it.

Do date your entries – sometimes you might want to read back through your journal or pick up an old one and browse through it. It's interesting to have a note of when you wrote that particular sentence or felt a certain way. Reading something you wrote two or ten years ago and realizing how far you've come since then can be empowering and extremely satisfying. Similarly, you might discover that you've been writing about a dream or goal since 1976 and still haven't got around to it. That just might be the push you need to go for it.

Reflection

Get started with your journal by writing about one thing in your life that gives you joy, one that concerns you and something that you would like to change. If you feel you cannot limit yourself to only one, even better!

Imagine your life as an hour glass – how full of sand is it? Write down the things that it is too late for, and the things that it is not time for yet. What is it time for now?

Look back over the last twenty-four hours of your life. What has gone well for you? What have you done well? What do you wish had not happened? What do you wish you had not done? How are you going to make tomorrow different from today?

Relationships 1: With People

With Those Left Behind

Only in the agony of parting do we look into the depths of love.

George Eliot

The young woman who was joining the party clung to her two children, telling them how she would see them soon and how good it would be when they met again. Finally she let her husband load them into the car, and as they drove off she waved until they were long out of sight. She turned to me with a sigh: 'Everything I love, everything that matters to me in the world, is in that car. I shall only be half alive until I see them again.'

Any journey involves leaving important relationships and familiar ties behind. Historically, this could be quite a formalized process. One fourteenth-century pilgrim, for example, had to obtain permission to journey from the lord of the village, and even from his wife! He also had to settle all his debts and make a will, knowing that he could die on his journey. Always in mind was not only the absence of those left behind for the year or so it took to make the journey to Santiago, Rome or Jerusalem, but the risk of never being reunited with them.

Today we're more accustomed to travelling, expect safe travel and are used to living with periodic absences. Nevertheless, that doesn't change the fact that journeying without the people to whom you are closest can be a time for intense reflection on those relationships. Missing their company can give an opportunity for appreciating what they bring to your life. Away from the difficulties of living in a relationship, those difficulties can be considered and evaluated.

Reflection

Think of a person with whom you have a close relationship at home. Pick up a pebble from the road that seems to you to reflect your relationship with them – is it smooth and shiny, easy to handle? Or is it battered and sharp, with rough edges?

Hold the pebble as you walk along, and hold that person in your heart. List their good characteristics. Remember occasions when their presence has given you joy. Forgive them for the wrongs and hurts they have done to you, and acknowledge the difficulties that have been caused by your own misdeeds. When you come to a suitable spot, put

the pebble down carefully, recognizing all that this
relationship means to you and giving thanks for it.

Reflection
If you could make one telephone call to someone
before you died, whom would you call and what
would you say to them? At your next opportunity,
make that call – why wait?

With Journey Companions

If nothing else, a road trip amounts to several
days of running conversation with friends, and
since good conversation is so hard to come by
these days, that in itself, is worth the effort.

John Gierach, from *Another Lousy Day in Paradise*

My son Simon had already annoyed the cyclist by tripping over his
obviously expensive bicycle on his way into the refuge. No doubt
Simon's inability to understand his rather broken and laborious
attempts at English further convinced the man that this boy was
scarcely worth the bunk space. This was reinforced by Simon's
backpack performing its usual trick of exploding on opening,
showering the entire floor with cutlery, laundry and half-drunk
bottles of Coke. A rather distant evening meal followed, then an
early night, because the day had been scorching and the journey
long and difficult.

In the morning, Simon was clearly still half asleep. Dragged out of bed before he was fully awake, he sat slumbering at the table, eyes half opened in the way that all teenagers are when they wish reality was something that happened to other people.

The cyclist opened one of his saddlebags, and extracted a single sachet of coffee. 'I will make you this. You will be fine.' He did, and Simon was. On leaving, the cyclist presented Simon with his last five sachets of coffee: 'Take these; you need them more than I do.'

Historically, pilgrims would travel with companions for safety. In the eleventh century only two or three travelling companions were deemed necessary. As time went on and the danger of brigands and accidentally walking into regional conflict increased, these two or three companions swelled to a significant number. By the fifteenth century – Chaucer's time – pilgrims travelled in large groups: sometimes entire trade's guilds or even villages departed together. As *The Canterbury Tales* amply demonstrates, a lot of the pleasure of the trip was derived from this companionship, and this is no less true today. Mingled with the excitement of an adventure was the sense that with all those features that defined and limited a personality left behind – social and marital status, past behaviour and present circumstances – a whole new person could be constructed.

Not all such groups were congenial, however. Margery Kempe was unusual both in that she was a female travelling without her husband and that she wrote of her experiences. Yet she seems to have been a very unpopular companion, due partly to her habit of befriending unpleasant characters and partly to the highly excitable nature of her spirituality – hours of loud sobbing were not uncommon. On one occasion she annoyed her travel companions so much they abandoned her completely, forcing her to rely on the kindness of a stranger to help her on her way.

Today many people still choose to make their pilgrimage in groups, whether setting out as in medieval times from the same community or joining a group of people with the same pilgrimage intention. They will journey the whole of the way with these people, and share with them a number of experiences, both good and bad. Through sharing this journey they will begin to see these companions in a different way, distinct from the selves that they show in their normal lives.

Even for those who choose to make their pilgrimage alone there will still be travelling companions. These are the people who are travelling the same route as you, but at a different speed, or in longer or shorter days of journeying. Relationships with these fellow travellers can be very intense and very rewarding. Many pilgrims have written about the way that those sharing a journey form a whole new community. Traditional ways of judging people no longer apply. Different criteria are used instead – how helpful a pilgrim is, how much they share both their knowledge and possessions. The best equipment, envy-provoking though it might be, will stand the surly or selfish pilgrim in no good stead when it comes to making space for them in a crowded refuge. The equality of the pilgrim is overlaid with a hierarchy reflecting the cheerfulness, helpfulness and openness to experience of each individual. Only by those are your contributions to the Way measured.

Reflection

Try to learn ten things you did not know before about your journey companion, through observing them and conversing with them. Reflect on these facts and how they alter your relationship. Think of ten good characteristics of your companion and find a way of sharing these with them, acknowledging what this relationship means to you.

Reflection

Companions you meet along the way may be no more than fleeting encounters, intense but brief. Make sure you have in your pack things that may be useful to a fellow traveller – needle and thread, blister plasters, cream for insect bites. Leave useful objects behind in the refuges that you use – a bowl of sweets, perhaps, or some fresh milk; things that will make the journey of those who follow you more comfortable.

With People on the Way

If you want others to be happy, practise compassion. If you want to be happy, practise compassion.

Dalai Lama

Although I thought I had planned my day's walk well, I had not walked as fast as I thought, so that by the time I reached the village it was after 12.30 p.m. and everything was shut. There are few sights that are bleaker to a pilgrim than a French village at midday. Doors were closed, windows shuttered, even the dogs and chickens that are so much a part of the pilgrim landscape had disappeared. I climbed wearily up the stairs into the church, whose mercifully open doors beckoned me into the cool interior. I sat for a while, looking at the peeling frescoes and smelling the damp air, then shouldered my pack once more.

Outside in the hot sun, waiting until I had finished in the church, was an elderly woman. Immaculately dressed and wearing a broad-brimmed hat, she held out a bottle of mineral water, so cold the condensation ran down the outside. 'Pilgrim?' she asked, and when I said yes, 'Is there anything you need? Can I help you in any way?' Gentle and gracious, she retreated when I said that I was all right and walked back up the path to the large manor house next to the church. I walked on, my heart lightened by this brief and generous meeting.

A pilgrim planning his a journey in the eleventh century might expect to pay at least a year's income. Although this was no problem for the wealthy, the poorer pilgrim had only two options. The best approach was to find a sponsor, someone who would benefit from the spiritual advantages of pilgrimage by sharing the cost. This method of vicarious pilgrimage – paying someone else to go on pilgrimage for you – was very popular, particularly if in a moment of extreme fear or illness, a wealthy man had made a vow to undertake a pilgrimage if he was spared. Often upon recovery the practical dangers and difficulties of such a task might easily induce a man to pay someone else to undertake the journey. If a patron could not be found, there was no alternative but to live rough and hope for alms.

Fortunately, pilgrims were thought to be deserving cases for charity, and were even exempt from the laws forbidding begging in towns that were passed at the end of the Middle Ages. According to one eighth-century text, a pilgrim was entitled to a roof over his head, a fire, wholesome water and fresh bread. On busy routes hospices were built to accommodate the vast numbers that passed by. They were basic places, often crowded, but still they provided much-needed shelter.

Today, travelling along the more popular pilgrim routes and bearing the now-international symbol of pilgrimage, the scallop shell, the pilgrim is easily recognized (see The Journey's End, page 122). But their status is a peculiar one. Freed from the contempt that is often accorded to the casual tourist by the locals, it is both easy and dangerous to take for granted the special status accorded to the spiritual traveller. It is important to remember that discounts, upgrades, concessions, privileges – all these things – bring merit to the donor and do not serve to raise the status of the recipient. The Confraternity of St James, the society set up to bring together people interested in the medieval pilgrim routes through France and Spain to Santiago de Compostela, is particularly strong on this point, as Laurie Dennett writes in *To Be a Pilgrim*: 'Tourists feel they have a "right" to expect this or that because they are paying for it; the condition of the pilgrim claims no "rights". The things of the Camino belong to each and every pilgrim, to the extent of taking responsibility for safeguarding them, but not in any personal, proprietary sense.' As it says on the door of a *refugio* in northern Spain: 'The tourist says "give me…" the pilgrim says "thank you".'

Reflection
Think of ways in which you can show your gratitude to the people who live along pilgrimage routes. As well as the obvious rules of 'taking only photographs, leaving only footprints', try to contribute to the community as well. If you can afford it, give donations to the local charities of villages you stay in. As well as leaving places tidy, try to make the task of those who clear up easier. For those who offer hospitality along the way, carry

small, attractive cards with a simple message of thanks printed on them. They need be no bigger than business cards, but if printed up before you begin your journey they can look good and help to indicate gratitude more easily in places where your language skills are not up to much!

Relationships 2: With Things

The High Importance of a Very Few Things

'Til taught by pain,
Men really know not what good water's worth;
If you had been in Turkey or in Spain,
Or with a famish'd boat's-crew had your berth,
Or in the desert heard a camel's bell,
You'd wish yourself where Truth is – in a well.

Lord Byron, *Don Juan* (Canto 2, 84)

It was Sunday lunchtime. The countryside lay quiet and still beneath a scorching sun. Although it was only just past noon, we decided to stop for lunch since we were so exhausted by the heat. But first we had to find water. The group of houses ahead was the last settlement for some miles, but it had no centre, no church and no water fountain. 'We'll have to knock on doors,' I said bravely. But for many houses we managed only to wake the dogs, and their furious barking echoed in the heat-baked silence. As we neared the last houses we were beginning to feel the touch of desperation. We knew we could not continue the journey without water, but had no idea how to obtain it. Then we heard the crunch of footsteps on gravel behind the neatly trimmed hedge of a small cottage. I opened the gate, and desperately and inarticulately asked if by any chance some of that water that was in the process of being poured so lavishly on the plants could be spared for us. With a smile, the elderly man undid the hose from the garden tap and allowed us to fill our bottles from it. Then, darting inside, he brought out a plastic bottle of water that had clearly been in the fridge, and gave that to us as well. Sitting beneath a tree on a patch of grass further on, we shared the best drink we had ever tasted!

For those seeking to reproduce the journeys of the original apostles of Jesus, travelling without worldly comforts and trusting in God to provide them with all that was needed for the journey ahead was part of the very fabric of pilgrimage. Those who depended on the charity of strangers obeyed the commands of Jesus, as well as did those who helped along the way. To depend on the charity of strangers not only meant that the pilgrim obeyed the commands of Jesus to his disciples, but also offered the opportunity of charitable deeds to those who provided for them. The earliest lodgings for pilgrims in the eighth and ninth centuries were usually under the auspices of the monasteries. Part of the role of the monastery was to provide for the poor, and a weary pilgrim could usually be sure of finding food, water and shelter under their roof. As the number of pilgrims increased, so buildings specifically for their care were established. Some of these provided hospitality to poor pilgrims who could pay nothing, and others, such as inns, charged a sum of money in return for food and lodging. However, on every major pilgrimage, there were still great stretches of the journey that lacked all but the most basic of help. Meseta, the famous plain that must be crossed on the journey to Santiago de Compostela, is known as a place of purification, as the landscape is so unrelieved by features that, however many miles one walks, it seems as if no progress has been made, and the distance between watering places is only just within the limits of journeying.

Fortunately, the modern pilgrim is better served in terms of supplies and accommodation, but even so there are stretches of journeys where good planning is needed if one is not to become short of food or, more importantly, water. These occasions remind us that when the basic necessities of life are lacking, the presence or absence of luxuries becomes extremely unimportant: the most sophisticated water-carrying system in the world becomes useless when it is empty. So too the search for accommodation, which can be particularly pressing on some of the more populous routes, can become so overwhelming as to consume all one's energy and attention – a useful reminder of how privileged we have become and how difficult it is to function as human beings when the elements that sustain life are in short supply.

Reflection

Pour two glasses of water and place them in front of you. Into one put three spoonfuls of mud or dirt and mix it round so that the water becomes contaminated and undrinkable. Now consider that one in five of the world's population does not have access to safe drinking water. Remember that if you have food in your pack, clothes on your back and a place to sleep you are richer than 75 per cent of the world. Spend some time thinking about this, and then, slowly and in deep gratitude, drink the glass of clean water.

The Unimportance of Many Things

We act as though comfort and luxury were the chief requirements in life, when all we need to make us really happy is something to be enthusiastic about.

Charles Kingsley

Don't store up treasures on earth! Moths and rust can destroy them, and thieves can break in and steal them. Instead, store up your treasures in heaven, where moths and

rust cannot destroy them, and thieves cannot break in and steal them. Your heart will always be where your treasure is.

Matthew 6:19–21

In every pilgrim hostel or refuge there will be a small pile of things left behind. Some of these things have been genuinely forgotten – my son remains unforgiven for leaving the small but gorgeous bottle of shower gel behind in one hostel, forcing us to spend the rest of the time washing our hair with Woolite. Others, however, have clearly been abandoned as the owner has realized that ounce for ounce, the object does not justify its inclusion in an overloaded backpack. Sad bundles of clothing, a worthy novel, dried-out make-up, these things force us to redefine what is of importance for our journey, and what is simply a vanity.

In some ways, the pilgrims of earlier times had it easier than we do today, since for the average peasant taking the trip of a lifetime, packing was not something that took a great deal of time. Many were used to possessing only one set of clothes, with a spare set for Sundays and festivals only if a significant degree of prosperity had been acquired. Jesus' command to the apostles before they set out on their wanderings not to take with them an extra shirt or pair of shoes for the journey could thus easily be adhered to. The traditional pilgrim's attire mentioned previously – tunic and cloak, with a hat to defend from the sun and a stick to defend from wild animals and bandits, finished off with a stout pair of boots – meant that the bag or scrip needed to carry only a few pence and the all-important letter of commendation that served as passport, health insurance and food ticket.

This pared-down existence, combined with a belief that something will turn up, and perhaps a readiness to accept whatever the journey held by way of risk or hardship, is less easily achieved by today's pilgrim. Distracted by innumerable websites and magazines offering the latest aids to comfort while journeying, it is easy to overload oneself, if not with personalized luggage straps, then with sophisticated navigation equipment or the ultimate 'wicking' shirt. But part of the excitement of the journey, part of its challenge and adventure, is paring ourselves down to the absolute minimum and seeing how well we survive. Do we have the same easygoing nature when the luxuries we have come to rely on are not available? Is our confidence in who we are and how we fit into the world maintained once we have divested ourselves of the status symbols of possessions? Sometimes pilgrimage can be a place to ask hard questions about oneself, and deal truthfully with the answers!

Reflection

Find an old container – a paper cup or a tin can perhaps – and some pieces of rubbish. Scatter them on the ground in front of you and look at the effect they have on the space. Spend some time thinking of the luxuries on this journey that you have had

*to do without – your favourite food, a television
programme, a shopping trip. Consider their effect on
your life and whether they are harmful or beneficial.
If they are harmful, pick up a piece of rubbish, name
the luxury and place it in the container. When you
have finished the exercise, look at the effect that
clearing the rubbish has had on your surroundings.
Think about this as you place the container in a bin.*

Storytelling

How Stories Reflect and Shed Light on Our Lives

Stories can conquer fear, you know. They can make the heart bigger.

Ben Okri

The year we went to Italy on pilgrimage, our youngest was just
over a year old. I strapped him firmly into his carrier, tied books
and toys to the frame and I walked like that for miles, revelling
in the feeling of his warmth against my back and his little
fat hands tapping my head as he asked for a story. As we
walked I recited all the old nursery tales to tell him: Jack and
the Beanstalk, the Three Bears, Cinderella. And as I talked
I noticed the rest of the family was listening and I began to
personalize the stories, incorporating bits of the lanscape we
passed through and the people we met, until the stories were
long and complex, rich with family meaning. Even now, four
years later, when I pick up one of those storybooks, my mind
is drawn immediately back to that time, and I recall the hot, dry

landscape we walked through and the sensation of tickly finders on my neck.

To the mostly mud-coloured world of the average medieval citizen, devoid of entertainment on all but the highest of festivals and feast days, stories and storytelling injected into the drabness a colour and energy that made things more bearable. But the stories of the saints that were handed down through the generations were more than just last-ditch attempts to quell the rising tide of boredom caused by endless days of living in the same small community. They shone a light into the lives of medieval people, and as we retell them today we learn something of their way of thinking, their hopes, their fears, and the way they strived and occasionally succeeded in making sense of the world around them. Pilgrims were themselves living out a story, reacting to and interacting with a tale that tried to explain the greater reality that surrounded theirs – an expression of salvation. By journeying to the sites associated with one of these lively, wholly human yet divinely favoured characters of the medieval calendar of saints – somewhere they lived, visited or were buried – the pilgrim was participating in the story of that saint, using it to explain his own life and take some meaning from it. It is not known whether they believed in the literal truth of these saints' lives, whether they used them as a metaphor for their own lives or as a way of articulating their powerlessness in the face of natural phenomena that were not understood, but it is certain that these tales provided another dimension to the lives of those who sought salvation through pilgrimage. Stories lead us out of the mundane; they inspire us to see more than the visible in the world.

We are more sceptical nowadays, taking unlikely tales of springs of holy water bubbling up where a man has been slaughtered for not renouncing his faith with little more than a pinch of salt. Yet it is doubtful whether society is any the richer for this: an acknowledgment of tales of supernatural events, of mysterious powers, of hidden realities that echo and enlighten our own reality can help us to find the universal in the particular. As we reflect on the similarities between stories from different times and different cultures, we relish the imagination and creativity that inspired them and find parallels within them for events in our own lives. And through our interaction with the stories of others, we can find, and make sense of, our own personal stories.

Reflection

Draw a patchwork quilt. Within each of the patches draw a significant event from your life or an episode from this pilgrimage. Decorate each patch if you can: colour it in or fill it with a pattern. When you have finished, look at its beauty, the complexity within its simple structure, and give thanks.

Solitude

Experiencing Solitude in an Overcrowded World

I restore myself when I'm alone.

Marilyn Monroe

I arrived at the hostel mid-afternoon – earlier than I was in the habit of doing, but this hostel had only five beds and I wanted to be sure that I got one of them. My heart sank when I entered the room – there was already another pilgrim there, busily rinsing some clothes in the sink. I had spent a long day walking, mostly uphill, and needed to rest, not socialize. The pilgrim gave a start of surprise when I came in, then a huge grin lit up his face, and he burst into a stream of rapid Spanish. Even my evident incomprehension did not throw him – he simply swapped languages and continued just as fast, although rather less accurately. He had been travelling for two days, cycling through the bleak countryside, and he had not spoken to a soul. He had spent the last two nights camping wild, and living off his emergency food supplies, as this was a very unpopulated region. Feeling rather like *Treasure Island*'s Jim Hawkins when the shipwrecked Ben Gunn chances upon him, I let the voice of the man wash over me as I sorted myself out. His initially wild-eyed expression gradually calmed down, and his sentences became slower, with pauses in between. By suppertime he had recovered his equilibrium, but in the morning I heard him making arrangements with a fellow cyclist to travel with him for the next leg of the journey – clearly enough was enough!

In the early days of pilgrimage, solitude was not something to be sought or desired. The single traveller, undefended and vulnerable, took his life into his hands when he set off upon pilgrimage. In theory his letter of commendation presented to him by a priest at the special pilgrim's mass held before his departure served also as a letter of safe conduct (see Leaving, page 24). Proof that the traveller was a genuine pilgrim meant that he enjoyed a greater measure of safety than other travellers by virtue of the severity of the punishments that awaited those who preyed on pilgrims. Every legal code had heavy penalties for those who attacked travellers, and from the early fourteenth century, molesters of pilgrims were included in the annual papal bull that listed the worst offences a person could commit. Yet even if they felt slightly safer than the ordinary traveller, pilgrims would never have been totally at ease. Groups of bandits lived by the sides of the major pilgrimage routes, regularly robbing pilgrims and on occasion leaving them without even the means to travel home. There is a church in

Boughton Aluph, ten miles from Canterbury, which has a large brick porch complete with a fireplace. It was here that pilgrims gathered until there were enough of them to journey in safety through the infamous King's Wood – haunt of bandits and cut-throats. Similarly, at inns and hostels in ports and at the beginning of pilgrim routes, single travellers would wait until they could join a group going the same way, as so famously described in Chaucer's *Canterbury Tales*, in which the travellers meet at an inn before deciding to journey together.

In contrast, solitude is one of the greatest experiences that a modern pilgrimage can offer, and the ability to survive alone one of its greatest gifts. In this overcrowded world, the individual is often lost in the crush of humanity that presses upon us on a daily basis. Although we may be spared the trauma of a commute into a large city, we may still encounter vast numbers of people in supermarkets or town centres and at events. Even if our daily lives do not provide much in the way of crowds, we will constantly be made aware that we are not alone. Sharing a home or an office with people brings with it its range of demands – some constant, some intermittent – provoking the need to react, respond and communicate. Television, radio, newspapers and other such media invite large numbers of people into our lives, to reflect and comment on them. Our sense of self can rapidly become merely a composite of other people's thoughts, reflections and expectations. A lengthy journey made completely or partly alone or in a small group can offer the space needed for pilgrims of today to make a parallel journey into their inner selves, to explore their psychological landscape in the midst of an unknown physical one, and to make new discoveries about each.

Reflection

On a large piece of paper draw your face – the face that you present to the world. Label your features to help you if you like – 'large smile, never letting anything get me down or upset me'. On the other side of the paper draw your face again – the face that you really are. Once again label your features to help you – 'small smile, often sad, frequently hurt by other people's comments'. Look at these two faces and think of ways in which you can make the two more similar.

Using Solitude

There are days when solitude, for someone my age, is a heady wine that intoxicates you with freedom, others when it is a bitter tonic, and still others when it is a poison that makes you beat your head against the wall.

Colette, *Freedom*

It was the first day of my first pilgrimage alone, and I was terrified. Before I had always travelled with at least one companion, and although their company was often irksome, there had always been someone around to argue about which path was correct, the name of the strange vegetable for sale in the local market, whether it was better to stop at this refuge or walk on to the next one. Now all these decisions would have to be made by myself. Instead of relying on others, my strength, my energy, my determination would have to be self-fuelled. If anything went wrong I would have to deal with it all by myself. For someone who had moved from a crowded childhood home straight into marriage and children of my own I could count on one hand the number of days I had spent totally alone. And now I was about to triple that! And then, suddenly, I was filled with a wonderful sense of freedom and excitement. For the first time I would not be answerable to or responsible for anybody at all. I could live to my own timetable – more than that, I could discover what my own timetable was! Although aware all the time of my emotional ties to those I had left behind, I was on an adventure of discovery, both physical and mental, and I determined to make the very best of it I could.

Throughout the history of pilgrimage, the renunciation of contemporary society has been a deep and powerful spiritual impulse, and a powerful motivating factor for many pilgrims. Many great ascetics and spiritual thinkers embraced pilgrimage as a means of abandoning the ties and constraints of society and travelling unimpeded into the depths of the soul in pursuit of truth and holiness. Imitating Jesus as he found comfort and strength from his retreats into the wilderness, the medieval pilgrim could follow the same route, seeking the same results.

Similarly, the pilgrim of today can seek solitude and use it wisely. But to be truly valuable, the experience of solitude must be embraced rather than escaped from. Always, the necessity for physical safety remains a priority – there are without doubt many places where it is unwise to travel alone. But within these constraints, there will still be the opportunity for travelling alone, even if this must be by special arrangement, perhaps agreeing with a companion to travel some distance apart for a period of time, meeting for refreshment and rest. If you are unused to spending time by yourself this can be a challenging task. Away from the people and occupations that can distract us from ourselves, away from day-to-day encounters with the world that takes place outside our beings, we can be frightened by the apparent wasteland that is our inner landscape. But before we can truly understand others, we must first understand ourselves. Prolonged periods of solitude will enable us to meet and understand properly who we are – perhaps for the first time in our lives.

Reflection

Take a piece of fruit and study it carefully. See how it is perfectly made for the function it has to perform. In what ways are you perfectly made for the things you do? What do you do that makes life sweeter for others? Consider in which areas of your life you are fruitful – how might you become more productive? In which areas are you fruitless, barren, producing nothing? Should these areas be pruned, cut away? Would this help you to grow more fully in other areas of your life?

Now eat the fruit and be thankful for it. Be thankful for your own self, for all you bring to the world that is unique and precious.

Penance

The Weight of Regret

But penance need not be paid in suffering... It can be paid in forward motion. Correcting the mistake is a positive move, a nurturing move.
Barbara Hall

I noticed the woman at the café because although she carried the scallop shell, symbol of pilgrimage, on her back, she did not appear to fit into the usual mould of pilgrims I had met so far. She was slender, her short grey hair stylishly cut; even her walking clothes looked more suitable for a stroll in the park than an arduous journey. She was drinking espresso, another trait seldom found in a pilgrim, since anything that risks dehydration is unwise, but clearly her former habits were still strongly engrained.

We began to talk, discussing the nature of the path and the challenges of navigation, especially if you are walking on your own and have no one to consider possibilities with. Then there was a silence and she said in her rather formal fashion: 'It's strange, you know, when I was married I longed for this sort of solitude, for the chance to make my own decisions, my own errors. Now I see perhaps I was wrong. I see a lot more things clearly, including the mistakes I have made. Not everything that happened was my fault, but perhaps more than I thought at the time.'

When I left her she was on her second cup of coffee, sitting motionless, looking out over the square, still thinking.

We have seen already that penance for sin was a key reason for undertaking pilgrimage in the Middle Ages. In a society where illness, accidents and unexplained evils were attributed to the sins of the unhappy victim, atoning for sin in order to avoid such punishment became almost an obsession. Gradually a conviction developed that a difficult and arduous journey, offered in a spirit of repentance, would placate a God angered by the sins a pilgrim had committed. This became more of an exact science as time went on, with particular routes for particular sins even being prescribed, and by the thirteenth century enforced pilgrimage had become, according to Sumption, 'the all-purpose penalty for violent crimes'. One of the most famous penitential pilgrims was Henry II, who went on pilgrimage to atone for the murder of Thomas à Becket, even making the last part of the journey on his knees.

Nowadays the fear of punishment, either in this world or the next, is not such a strong impulse for those embarking on a pilgrimage – although there are exceptions. A Belgium initiative, *Oikoten*, uses pilgrimages as part of its rehabilitation programme for young offenders. A 'long-term uprooting project', as it is called, brings many advantages, in the experience of the programme's organizers: 'You could describe it as creating a hiding place, with restricted limits in time and place, where youngsters get the possibility to practise taking responsibility for themselves and learn to take their future in their own hands. To reach the goal of their project, they have to make great efforts, every day. The rhythm or even the routine of walking or working makes all of them think about themselves, their past and their future, willing or not.'

For those not walking the path as part of a programme of rehabilitation, there can still be advantages to a period of reflection on past mistakes. Undertaking part of the journey in an attitude of repentance can lead to a transformed view of one's own past and a new way of behaving in the future. Travelling in a penitential way should not involve additional discomfort – the journey will probably be hard enough as it is – but ways of encouraging a penitential mind can be found. The journey can be an opportunity to find new ways forward with ourselves, with others and with the world at large.

Reflection
Think about your attitude to yourself. Perhaps you have been hurt in the past so often that you are afraid to be vulnerable. Perhaps you have stopped taking risks for fear of pain; you have become closed against the world, sceptical about what it has to offer. A cynical attitude can be harmful to the personality that carries it as well as to

*your companions. Clench your hands into fists, as tightly
as you can. Walk along the road for half a kilometre
with them like this, symbolizing a soul clenched against
the world. Notice what an effort it takes to keep them
clenched, the amount of energy you are expending. Now
stop and, taking deep breaths, turn round in a full circle,
looking all around you. Slowly unclench your fists, unfold
your hands and open your heart to the world. Walk more
slowly for a while, noticing the effect this has on you.*

Reflection

*Think about your attitude to other people, especially
ways in which you have hurt or offended them.
Pick up a small stone or a stick, and carry it with
you as you walk. Notice how irritating it is to carry
this object, how it stops you moving your arms
comfortably. Reflect on how your behaviour to
others might have seemed just like this object – not
dangerous in itself, but irritating and annoying.
Think of particular characteristics or mannerisms
you may have that make the lives of others run less
smoothly. Drop the object, and with it drop whatever
character traits you have discerned in yourself that
cause distress to others.*

Reflection

*Think about your attitude to creation. Walk more
slowly for the next half-kilometre, taking time to
look around you at the landscape. Reflect not only*

on the wonderful, beautiful aspects of creation, but on the way that human beings have changed and marred their surroundings. When you come to a populated section of the journey, take an old carrier bag and spend a morning litter-picking as a way of doing penance for your own part in the destruction of the landscape.

Burdens

Letting Go of Unnecessary Burdens

For the poison of hatred seated near the heart doubles the burden for the one who suffers the disease; he is burdened with his own sorrow, and groans on seeing another's happiness.

Aeschylus

I knew something was bothering the woman as I watched her fiddling with her mobile phone: putting it first in one pocket, then the next, changing the volume of the ring tone, examining it frequently to check it had a good signal. When our paths fell in together for a few days I discovered why. This was her first pilgrimage and, more significantly, her first time away alone since her children had been born. She had left them with her husband, who seemed to need constant instruction and reassurance in order to manage the most basic tasks. Our walk was punctuated by the woman's rather desperate answers to his continuous queries – how to put the washing machine on, what to cook for lunch, how to discipline the youngest who was not adjusting well to the regime change... She looked worn out and her enjoyment of the journey was clearly only partial – most of her heart and spirit was back at home.

Our paths diverged for about a week as we took different routes, but some days later I saw Domestic Woman again, looking completely different. Gone was the constant slight frown between her brows; she was no longer so agitated – she looked full of joy. I asked her how her journey had been, interested to discover what had effected this transformation. The answer was simple – she had travelled through an area where there was no phone reception. Out of touch for four days, she had first agonized, then accepted, the inevitable. When she finally got a signal on her phone, the situation at home had also changed dramatically. No longer able to get constant advice, the husband had discovered how to manage for himself. The anxious phone calls were no longer, and each party could enjoy their own circumstances.

There were always clerics and writers who strongly disapproved of pilgrimage, even when its popularity was at its height. Indeed, by the end of the fifteenth century, there was a strong feeling that most people went on pilgrimage for light-hearted and frivolous reasons, with most pilgrims distinctly lacking the spiritual fervour and intensity of their ancestors. To the inhabitant of the modern world, this feeling is entirely understandable. The average member of the lower classes would have very little opportunity for travel and diversion in the ordinary course of his life. Confined to his village by the monthly round of agricultural tasks, even a trip to the local town was a rarity. An opportunity to escape one's obligations and duties, to throw off the burdens of everyday life, was not to be passed by lightly. In addition to this, life on the road often lacked the normal restraints of daily life. Comments from as early as the fourth century and as late as the fifteenth portray the licentiousness and bawdiness of some groups of travelling pilgrims. Some travellers clearly found the journey so entertaining compared to the monotony of life in the village that they never returned home but stayed on the road – perpetual pilgrims.

Although most of us nowadays recognize that pilgrimage can be but a brief opportunity to escape the burdens and routines of everyday life, this can nonetheless be a very valuable opportunity. Away from the pressure of daily habits, an opportunity may arise to reflect on and perhaps reassess those aspects of our lives that we find burdensome. Pilgrimage can be a time for looking at relationships and our role within them, for exploring the motivations behind the tasks we undertake even though we find them debilitating and depressing, for examining other paths in life besides those along which we are currently walking. Use the time of your pilgrimage to re-examine your life, and consider some of those things that can be changed or let go. Are they burdens because you want them to be, because you gain self-definition from them? Are they burdens from habit, because you have never really examined why you carry them? Are they not your burdens at all, but those of someone else, which you are carrying for them?

Reflection

Take a large sheet of paper and in the centre, draw an empty piece of luggage. It could be the backpack or suitcase you have with you at the moment, or another piece. Around the outside of your luggage draw various items of clothing, food and accessories that you might want to take on a journey. Now think of those things in your life that you consider to be burdens – things whose weight can sometimes be hard to carry. Assign each of your burdens to a piece of packing, according to their importance and seriousness. So, a young child or a dependent relative could be a tent or sleeping bag. A commitment to a monthly meeting could be an item of clothing. A friend whose company you find difficult might be represented by something smaller, such as a spare toothbrush! Once you have done this, decide which items you definitely need to take with you on your life's journey, and draw them inside your luggage.

When your piece of luggage is full, stop drawing. Look at what you left out – can these be given to others to carry or help to carry? Better still, can they be left behind? If you put all your items in, repeat the exercise!

Bearing the Necessary Burdens

Respect the burden.

Napoleon Bonaparte

For the first time on a pilgrimage, I was not relying on hostels or inns. Trying to free myself from the tyranny of arriving at a certain place at a certain time, I had bought a tent. It was a good one – sturdy, yet as light as possible, with every weight-saving device there was. Even so, it weighed six pounds, and when I strapped it to the top of my pack I was certainly aware it was there. We were walking in a fairly mountainous region, and the extra weight of the tent soon made itself felt. I found myself resenting the tent, thinking how much easier my walk would be if I did not have to carry it, questioning the wisdom of my decision to bring it with me. Then one morning I decided to try a different approach. Before I took it down after the night's camp, I walked all round it, admiring it, appreciating the good night's sleep I had had in it, valuing its design and structure. I packed it up and strapped it on, determining not to resent it for its additional load, but to appreciate it for the freedom it brought. It seemed lighter, and over the days to come it became almost animate in my mind – a shelter, a protection, a trusted companion in my travels.

Sometimes the burdens we bear are not of our own making, nor do we have a choice about whether we carry them or not. For the medieval pilgrim, gender might have been one such burden. From the very beginning, pilgrimage was thought by some people to be an inappropriate occupation for women. St Boniface (AD 680–754) believed that female pilgrims sacrificed their virtue by engaging in pilgrimage. Centuries later Thomas More commented on the behaviour of women pilgrims who sang obscene songs while journeying. Margery Kempe gives in her diaries an account of the treatment of women pilgrims by their companions. She was mocked for her piety, her goods were stolen and on some pilgrimages she was even abandoned (see Relationships 1, page 44). However, she continued to travel widely throughout England and further afield, trying to complete her journeys in a pious and prayerful way, despite the difficulties she so often encountered.

The modern pilgrim may also carry burdens that cannot be easily shed – and perhaps should not. It might be a physical condition, painful or uncomfortable, that limits our life. The burden of mental illness, of depression or anxiety may make participation in everyday life more difficult than it is for others. We may have people who rely on us to look after them – small children or elderly and sick relatives. We may simply be financially responsible for others, unable to live as we choose because of our obligations. These things can be hard to bear, and can be made almost unbearable if our attitude to them is grudging or angry. Pilgrimage is an opportunity to reflect on those parts of our lives over which we have little or no control, to acknowledge the impact they have on us and perhaps to come to a deeper acceptance of the limitations they place on us, with recognition of the advantages they can also bring.

Reflection

Look at the drawing you have made of your piece of luggage, filled with objects. One by one, examine these objects, symbols of the necessary burdens you have to carry. Try to appreciate the benefits they can bring. Reflect on what you have learnt from carrying this burden, what gifts of understanding or sympathy for others have been given to you through this burden. For each object, try to find something to be thankful for. Finally, tear the paper round the edge of the luggage, leaving behind those things you did not include inside the bag, and place your drawing in an inner pocket of the backpack or bag that you are using on this journey as a symbol of your acceptance of your life's burdens and recognition of the good that can be seen in them.

Healing

Cured or Healed?

The miracles of the church seem to me to rest not so much upon faces or voices or healing power coming suddenly near to us from afar off, but upon our perceptions being made finer, so that for a moment our eyes can see and our ears can hear what is there about us always.

Willa Cather, from *Death Comes for the Archbishop*

For as long as I had known the woman she had suffered from backache. In the winter months it grew quite severe, and even during the summer it never went totally away. Refusing medical investigation, she relied on painkillers to get her through the bad times and stoicism when the ache was less acute. Mother of a young family, always busy, her decision to spend part of her holiday on a walking pilgrimage surprised me. I wondered how she would manage to walk such long distances with a heavy pack on her back. Evidently she did too, as during the following weeks I watched her trying to train for the walk, trailing her children with her as she set off along the footpaths.

But walk she did, and returned looking years younger. When I asked her how her back had been, she replied with a delighted smile that it was almost completely cured. Years of carrying a child on one hip had strained her muscles. A lengthy period of time without children, combined with the muscle-building exercise of walking long distances with an evenly placed – if heavy – load had gone a long way toward solving her problem. 'I never went looking for a cure, only an adventure,' she told me, 'but I am so glad that I found both!'

In February 1858 a fourteen-year-old girl named Bernadette Soubirous received the first in a series of visions of the Virgin Mary near her home in Lourdes, France. After the first recognized healing took place at Lourdes in March of the same year the prestige of the place as a site for healing grew rapidly, increasing with the advent of railways, so that by the end of the century visitors numbered hundreds of thousands – 30,000 were recoded in August 1897 alone.

As mentioned previously, pilgrimages that seek healing – both through the journey itself and by visiting a shrine – are perhaps one of the most consistent kinds of journey through the centuries, continuing even when pilgrimage was otherwise in decline (see Leaving, page 21). In understanding this we have to remember that until relatively recently so many and varied were the illnesses that afflicted the vast majority of people during their lives that likely few people ever felt completely well. Jonathan

Sumption has argued that many of the problems were dietary – even in times of good harvest, the average diet was prone to deficiencies. During the winter, shortage of fresh fruit and vegetables brought a lack of vitamin C that showed itself in muscle pain and even scurvy, while a shortage of vitamin A might lead to bladder problems, skin infections or eye problems. Found in dairy products and fish, these were scarce commodities in towns in the summer months. Digestive problems were commonplace, as were diseases caused by poor sanitation. It is not surprising then that the search for a cure was often a strong motivating factor, and the popularity of some sites grew ever greater with the news of miraculous healing accorded to suffering pilgrims circulating among the general population. Indeed it is quite possible that many of these cures were genuine, even if some of them may not have been long-lasting. Interestingly, the illnesses caused by dietary shortages in one area of the country could be cured simply by moving to a part of the country where that food was in plentiful supply; thus the pilgrimage itself provided the miracle that was sought. A prime example of this is ergotism, whose symptoms of gangrene, burning sensation in the limbs and convulsions were caused by eating rye infected by a certain type of mould, triggered by wet harvest conditions. A pilgrimage to a drier climate, eating uninfected rye, could cause an almost instant end to this illness. Despite this, tales of miraculous cures and healings abounded, with certain sacred sites becoming associated with cures for specific diseases. A sufferer of toothache could travel to St Hugh's shrine in Lincoln, for example, or if the problem was with the eyes a journey to St Candida's well in Dorset might cure the problem. If you had leprosy, then a longer journey was necessary – perhaps to the shrine of St Lazare at Autun.

Alongside the belief that fervent prayer at the shrine of a particular saint might evoke the saint's pity and prompt a cure went the idea that physical illness was a sign of spiritual malady: illness was caused by the sufferer's sin, or was even a punishment from the saint for a certain offence. Prayer at this saint's shrine would bring reprieve.

Whatever one's take on miraculous healings, it is certain that many medieval pilgrims believed strongly in the healing power of pilgrimage and penitence, to such an extent that often a cure was effected, if not by the miraculous intervention of the saint then by the power of the mind over the body – in itself a sort of miracle.

Nowadays, there are fewer pilgrimages made for the sole purpose of seeking physical healing, though Lourdes has retained its popularity, with 200 million pilgrims having visited the site to date and 4,000 cures certified by the Bureau de Constation. In a smaller way, the country church of Pennant Melangell (home of St Melangell), restored in 1150, was for some time a site of pilgrimage for the sick and diseased. Falling into disuse, it was again restored in 1992 and developed into a centre for healing, with a respite care unit for cancer sufferers. In 2003 it changed its name to The St Melangell Centre, with a broader remit to support adults with emotional, spiritual and mental health needs. There may be a degree of scepticism about these claims of cures and healing, but as the Bishop of Tarbes and Lourdes says: 'The current attitude of doctors is very respectful of the Magisterium of the Church. As Christians, they know that a miracle is a spiritual sign. They don't want to be judges on this matter. Moreover, for a modern mentality, it is difficult to say that something is "inexplicable". They can only say that it is "unexplained".'

Far more common, however, is the notion that the healing – more spiritual and emotional than physical perhaps – lies in the journey itself. Time out from the daily routine and freedom from the stresses and responsibilities of everyday life can give the modern pilgrim opportunities to reflect on their spiritual and emotional wellbeing and find ways of working towards a state that is not necessarily a cure, but that more valuable gift, a healing.

Reflection

Find a seed and a small patch of earth. Examine the seed – it is full of potential. Dormant inside is new life and growth. But in order to grow, to become what it is fully meant to be, it must be planted deep into cold, dark earth. It is only after having spent time in the dark, motionless and still, that it will be able to move and grow towards the light. As you plant the seed in the patch of earth, reflect on aspects of your life at the moment that are dark and still, perhaps

*full of pain and suffering. Think of ways in which new
life might be able to spring from these difficult times,
redeeming them and making them fruitful. If you
cannot think of anything positive that may yet spring
from the darkness, remember that just as we have
to trust that the seed, once planted, will germinate
and grow, so we too in times of despair may have the
seeds of new light and hope growing within us. We
just can't see them yet.*

Reflection

*Find some bits of broken tiles or glass. Try to get as
many different types and colours as possible, but
remember to take care that they are not sharp or
contaminated. Carefully place these broken pieces on
the ground until, together, they form a new shape – a
circle, which is whole and new. Reflect that although
the pieces of your life that are broken and shattered
may not be able to be as they were, they can be put
together in a new way to form a new wholeness, with
the pain of the individual experience assimilated in
the beauty of the whole.*

Living for the Moment 1: Awareness of Self

Becoming More Aware of Our Physical Selves

If anything is sacred, the human body is sacred.

Walt Whitman, from *Leaves of Grass*

I had noticed the pilgrim earlier on the journey, or rather, I had noticed his kit. Near the beginning of a pilgrimage route, it is easy to distinguish those who have undertaken this sort of journey before – their packs are weary and battered, either with bits and pieces dangling from every spare inch of the outside, or with everything stowed away, not a thing to be seen. The kit of a seasoned traveller is highly idiosyncratic as well – some items are obviously top of the range, acquired as the pilgrim has realized what is vital for his comfort; other parts are shabby, contrived or manufactured out of something rather peculiar but which nonetheless 'does the trick'. This pilgrim, however, was clearly a 'newbie' – and no ordinary newcomer to the game either. Every single piece was top of the range, very expensive, ultra light, micro fibre – if you had ever drooled over it in a kit catalogue, he had it in his pack. As he set off the next morning I heard mutterings from the other travellers – mostly envious. I myself thought that for someone with such excellent kit, he seemed curiously weighed down with it, his gait unstable and uneven.

A few stages later I met him again. I had already arrived at the refuge when he staggered in, white-faced. The day's walk had been long, but not excessive, so I thought at first he might be ill. Then he sat down and slowly and tenderly unlaced his boots and peeled off his socks. The sight of his feet made us both blench. Large blisters had clearly formed, then burst, then bled. One of his toenails had turned black with bruising, the tops of his other toes chafed raw by the boots. 'New boots,' groaned the man. 'Big mistake,' I answered. The evening was spent helping the pilgrim to clean up his feet and discussing patent foot remedies with other pilgrims as they wandered in: sheep's wool, thick socks, lots of socks, blister pads, white spirit – all were discussed, but clearly this man's feet had gone beyond preventative measures. The following day I walked with him to the station and left him, disconsolate, his feet resting on his brand new, and still unused, pack.

The medieval pilgrim might have been both fitter and less fit than we are today. Certainly many of them would have had manual jobs, and been used to the rigours of hard physical labour in all sorts of conditions. Indeed an agricultural labourer might have found a pilgrimage to be some sort of physical holiday, with the only thing asked of him to walk steadily in one direction. Each month of the year had its clearly defined agricultural tasks, whether pushing a plough through thick, sticky soil (or, for the luckier ones, walking over the land guiding the beasts as they ploughed), or performing the many backbreaking tasks associated with crop-growing: picking out stones, hoeing and harvesting. However, although in his youth this work might have made him fit and full of energy, years of unending labour would have put stresses and strains on his body that may have made him vulnerable to injury. Added to that the various illnesses caused by poor diet, and the aspiring medieval pilgrim may not have been in such good shape after all!

The journey itself would take a toll on the body. The skeleton of a pilgrim found buried under the floor of Worcester Cathedral shows the effect of long-distance walking on the body – he had suffered from arthritis so badly that it had fused some of the bones of his spine and ribcage. His right shoulder had suffered from inflammation – archaeologists speculate that the constant lifting and placing down of his staff not only gave him well-developed right arm muscles, but also arthritis in his shoulder. His feet too had become malformed after walking long distances.

If you decide to undertake a pilgrimage on foot, it might be the single most demanding piece of physical exercise you ever take. Very often we remain unaware of our bodies in our day-to-day lives, noticing them only when they temporarily cease to function. Aware that we should take some exercise – usually guiltily aware that we don't take quite enough – we must be very serious about training and preparing for the journey if our bodies are not to let us down before the experience has properly begun. A programme of regular walking, leading to two- and three-day expeditions wearing all the kit that you will wear on your journey, will help acclimatize you to the stresses and strains your body must expect.

However, nothing can really prepare you for the experience of walking for long periods of time, day after day. Even well-worn boots can rub, and even the friendliest and most ergonomic pack can cause backache! Care must be taken to adjust slowly to the demands of pilgrimage – planning too long a stage at the beginning can result in a journey cut abruptly short through injury.

The physical benefits of pilgrimage will soon become apparent, however. A complete dependence on your physical condition will make you grateful for your body and aware of your reliance on its performance in a way that is quite unique. New muscles being felt for the first time, a sense of growing in fitness and a huge feeling of physical wellbeing, uncomplicated and direct, can be liberating and exciting. Moments of feeling totally at one with your physical self, conscious of each part carrying out its task as it is supposed to, will more than compensate for the aching feet and tired legs that all pilgrims are prone to.

When walking and resting, take time out to be aware of your body, to celebrate it and be grateful even for the parts you don't particularly like! Feeling good in your skin is a gift from the road – enjoy it.

Reflection

Do this exercise at the end of the day, when you have taken off your walking shoes and socks and your feet are clean. Or do it when you come to a stream. Take time out to wash them in the clear water, refreshing and energizing them. Take a large piece of paper and place it on the ground and stand on it. If you don't have any paper, clear a patch of ground and draw a square just big enough to stand in. Then look at your feet. Be aware of every bump and irregularity. Admire your toes! Slowly relax every part of your foot, starting with your toes, then moving to your arches, your ankles. Think of where they have taken you, both before your pilgrimage and now on your journey. Think of the steps you have taken together. Before you move on, feel how firmly you are standing, and resolve to continue to do so.

Learning to Live in the Moment

There exists only the present instant... a Now which always and without end is itself new. There is no yesterday nor any tomorrow, but only Now, as it was a thousand years ago and as it will be a thousand years hence.

Meister Eckhart

Seize the day.

Horace, *Odes* (1.11)

The man was a real map junkie. Everyone spends some time in the evenings looking to see where they have journeyed, planning the next stage, trying to commit the major points of the next day's route to memory, but this man took it to extremes. Every minute of his rest time was spent gazing at the map – he even read it in bed, and as soon as he stepped out in the morning he was once again engrossed in study. He was also concerned with the minute details of how far he had travelled and how long it had taken. He would quiz other pilgrims on the length and timing of their journey, obligingly working out the number of miles they walked per hour – always less than you think it should be! Curiously, he did not seem to be enjoying himself. Instead, he looked on the pilgrimage as a task that had to be accomplished in a certain way, to a fixed timetable. He took planned breaks at predefined intervals for a specific amount of time, no matter what the weather was like, how beautiful the countryside, how appealing the local market.

I would like to say that he experienced an epiphany, a changing moment, when he realized how much he was missing through his obsession with time and route. But as far as I know he did not. I am sure he finished his pilgrimage on time as planned. But I wonder how much he gained from it.

For hundreds of years, 'mechanical time' did not exist for most people. Instead time was a much looser concept. Days ran from sunrise to sunset, with a break approximately in the middle to eat; seasons were from equinox to solstice, the waxing and waning of the moon, seedtime to harvest – an endless circle of days, punctuated by occasional festivals. The church had more of a grip on time, marking it out with saints' days and the liturgical year. Monasteries too punctuated the day with prayer. At certain times throughout the day the bell would toll and all would gather to remember their Creator. Even those who were unaffected by the daily office would hear the bell and pause for a moment.

To go on pilgrimage was to take an even greater break from time. The seasons affected how easy or hard the walk would be, whether baking in the sun or drowned out by the rain. The time of day was important since it was necessary to be in a safe place by nightfall, preferably having eaten, but there were no other fixed points. A pilgrimage took as long as it took (after all, there was a significant danger of never returning at all), and after that it was time to go home.

Nowadays, unless we are careful, we can fall into the trap of measuring out our journey into days, miles, stopping places, hours, even minutes. On pilgrimage, if nowhere else, it is vitally important to put aside such constraints if we are truly to allow ourselves to participate in the experience as fully as we can, to immerse ourselves in our journey, both physical and spiritual. It is of the utmost importance to make the most of now. Everything is sacred on pilgrimage, nothing more so than time – we must not desecrate it in a hurry. It is our task to look for the sacred in the ordinary, to relish every moment, to savour every meeting, every encounter, every experience.

To undertake a sacred journey such as a pilgrimage is to allow yourself time to think, to reflect, to listen to the lessons of the past and integrate them into a vision for the future. But that is only part of the task. The other part, which must provide the balance if the journey is to heal, nurture and develop the pilgrim, is to learn to live totally in the moment. On pilgrimage you must look and really see, listen and truly hear, eat and extract all the taste that is contained in the food. True freedom lies in learning to pay attention to the infinite detail that makes up each moment of our lives, allowing us to experience them in a new way. Our mindfulness enables us to live each day, each hour, as a new beginning, and to continue to face the future with an open heart and mind.

Reflection

*Find a stream of running water, take off your boots
and socks, and stand in the middle of the stream.
Hold your hands out in front of you, palms upward,
and spend some time just feeling the rushing of water
over your feet, cooling, cleansing. Allow it to refresh
your soul as well as your body. Become completely
aware of yourself as you live totally in this moment.
Turn to face downstream. Let the water flow past
you and away, taking with it bad memories of the
past, old grudges, past guilt and regrets. Let the
water wash through you, clearing away the rubbish
of your life, leaving you open and clean. Turn to face
upstream. As the water flows towards you think how
it brings with it new opportunities, new challenges,
new gifts. Some of these things you will have to let
flow past you; some you can accept and absorb. Now
feel yourself fully in the present once more, alive in
every part of you to every fraction of this experience.
Be thankful.*

Living for the Moment 2: Awareness of Surroundings

Experiencing Creation

**To see a world in a grain of sand
and heaven in a wild flower
Hold infinity in the palm of your hand
and eternity in an hour.**

William Blake, from 'Auguries of Innocence'

The American family was an uncomfortable addition to the refuge. Arriving late, they seemed to suck up any spare space, leaving the room feeling cramped and ungenerous. Their large packs only echoed their stature – the woman towered above the other women in the refuge and even some of the men. The men, a father and a son, were sulky and sullen – the boy did not speak at all. In a hushed whisper over the washing-up the other pilgrims shared fragments of the story of the family: the words 'drugs' and 'drink' and 'in with the wrong crowd' hung in the air, increasing the sense among the group of 'pilgrimage as punishment'. As the other pilgrims went up to the dormitory, the boy was left behind, glowering behind a tattered copy of a Spanish motorcycle magazine that was clearly his favourite companion on the journey.

I did not see the family again on the journey, as I was walking alone and quite rapidly, unencumbered by a reluctant teenager and his hormones. It was not until the airport, waiting for the flight out, that I spotted them in the distance – or at least I thought I did, because the family was almost unrecognizable. Relaxed and laughing, they seemed to form a close-knit group of companions. Catching up with the mother in a coffee queue I asked her how the trip had been. She radiated happiness: 'It was our last chance to get him to see sense,' she said. 'I thought we had blown it. But as we walked the miles and miles, through that glorious countryside, something stony inside him seemed to soften and melt in the sun. I have got my boy back, and I never thought I would.'

We have been reflecting on the fact that for many medieval pilgrims life was spent in the same place they were born, got married and died, and a pilgrimage was a huge undertaking. Living in tiny settlements, the number of people they would know would be small, but they would have intimate knowledge of them and their lives. The landscape that surrounded them would be just as familiar; most of it would have been walked over, cultivated, studied for signs of growth and change many times during the course of a lifetime. Even for town-dwellers, the landscape would be very well known, with every street walked down and every house a familiar sight. To leave the place of their home, their origins, and step out into unknown territory was an immensely brave thing to do. Possessing no maps, the pilgrim would rely on the knowledge of others to help him on his way. He could ask the inhabitants of each settlement where the path led to next. He could walk with companions who had travelled the path before, merchants who used the pilgrim routes to travel from place to place, messengers, itinerant workmen or beggars. But away from the houses he would have to rely on the signs of the landscape, looking for paths around natural obstacles such as rivers, trying to discern which was the best, shortest and safest route. The countryside could be beautiful, but it could be dangerous as well: flooded rivers and parched plains, thick forests inhabited by wild beasts and bandits, mountain ranges and hills – each would have to be travelled through, looking out for places to find water and food and somewhere to shelter when it grew dark or the weather grew fierce.

For most people today, our relationship with the landscape is not so intense. We are sheltered from the worst that nature has to offer, but sadly, often the best as well. With maps and guidebooks to show us the most efficient and easiest way, with signage improving rapidly, and if all else fails, rapid assistance at the end of a mobile phone, our lives no longer depend on the correct reading of the landscape surrounding us. But for all that, our relationship with the landscape we are journeying through is important and can teach us in all sorts of ways. The effect of the weather upon our sense of wellbeing, the way the slightest change of temperature can make a particular stage of the journey easy or difficult, the echoing of the external surroundings with our own internal landscape – all should be noted and reflected upon. Take time to walk slowly, to experience every aspect of the landscape you are travelling through – the effect of the light upon the trees, the roughness of the path, the incredible detail of the plants that surround you. Months later, when your pilgrimage is over, you will be able to recapture these feelings of intensity, of awareness of the landscape, of being an integral part of the created world.

Reflection

Find a leaf. Pick it up and spend some time studying it carefully. Look at the tracery of veins that spread out from the central stalk, reminding yourself of how this is mirrored in the vaulted ceilings of the churches and cathedrals you have visited. Examine its many lines of symmetry – and of asymmetry. See how the tiny imperfections of the leaf, those that make it different from the other leaves around, do not mar its appearance but contribute to its uniqueness. Reflect on the infinite detail that is present in this tiny fraction of the natural world. Remember the complexity of structure that undergirds this leaf – the cells and their components, the magnitude of the task that they perform so necessary for the health of the tree. Small and delicate, this leaf is apparently insignificant, yet completely perfect, beautiful and totally adapted for its task. So are you.

Obstacles on the Journey

The Obstacle of Fear

Courage is resistance to fear, mastery of fear, not absence of fear.

Mark Twain

For a long time I had wondered what was wrong with me – every time I set out to climb a mountain I would be filled with a huge fear. My stomach would churn, my legs would feel weak – I did not think I would make it out of the car park, let alone up the slopes. I did not really understand why this should be so – I had years of climbing experience, but each time I wondered whether this would be the time when I had an accident, or could not make the descent, or any one of a hundred disasters would befall me. I spoke about this to an experienced soldier. 'That's very common,' he said. 'Some of the young officers are physically sick before they set off on exercise, they are so scared. Even the older ones are nervous. It's a good sign – if you are not nervous, you probably aren't treating it seriously enough!'

For the English pilgrim travelling to Santiago, Rome or Jerusalem, the dangers started with the sea voyage. Although pilgrim ships were given licences to carry only certain numbers of pilgrims, many more were often smuggled aboard. Overcrowding made conditions unsanitary and unhealthy – disease spread quickly and seasickness became a major threat to life. Storms at sea often led to pilgrims committing themselves to yet another pilgrimage, if only they survived this one!

Once on dry land, pilgrims faced further dangers. The threat from wild animals in some of the less populated parts of the countryside was very real – one of the reasons for the pilgrim's staff. Outbreaks of plague along the way, or even viruses, to which passers-by were not immune, added the danger of illness. The threat from bands of robbers who preyed on the usually poorly equipped, unprotected groups of pilgrims meant that even if they walked in large groupings they ran a great risk of being robbed and attacked, or even abducted. Not even the law or papal disapproval could offer assurance of safe travel.

Although the dangers faced today by pilgrims are significantly fewer, it is nonetheless a decision of great courage to commit yourself to a journey of some length, without many of the modern comforts and conveniences we take for granted. Of course there are still some dangers along the road – being chased by large, fierce dogs is an almost daily occurrence along some routes! The risk of falling ill is also still present, particularly with stomach complaints if you are unused to the food of the region, and while pilgrims are less in danger from bands of marauding robbers, there are monuments along every major pilgrim route to those who have lost their lives in traffic accidents. Do not think this is a journey to be undertaken lightly: at times it will present challenges – both physical and mental – that are quite severe. How you face up to them will determine how much you will allow the journey to change you, how much you will grow and be transformed by your time on the road.

Reflection

Find somewhere quiet and secluded, where you can be sure of remaining undisturbed for as long as you want. Rather than let your fears scramble around in your head, try to write them down as a list. Study this list and see how you feel about your fears now – sometimes even the act of writing them down in an ordered way can diminish the power they have over you. Now select one fear that still grips your stomach when you think about it. Write this fear on the top of a clean sheet of paper. Beneath it write how this fear affects your life and your behaviour. Try to write down how you might feel if you did not have this fear: how you would behave and how it would affect your life. Scrunch the paper up in your hands, while you determine to act as if you were free of this fear and behave as if you were well able to deal with the things that make you afraid.

Reflection

Find a pile of stones of different sizes and shapes.
Pick up each stone, and describe out loud one of
your fears for this journey. Place the stone in a bag
or container of some sort. When you have named
all your fears and placed the corresponding stones
in the bag, lift up the bag and walk with it a short
way. See how heavy it is and how it is preventing
you from moving easily and acting as normally and
freely as you should. Empty out the stones by the
side of the road – build a cairn with them if you like.
Now move on, and as you leave behind the physical
embodiment of your fears, resolve also to leave
behind the fears themselves.

The Obstacle of Worry

**Worry does not empty tomorrow of its
sorrow. It empties today of its strength.**

Corrie Ten Boom

It was early in the morning and we were walking along a
particularly bleak part of the route. My teenage son was walking
with me. It had been very hot the day before and we were
tired; looking at the route guide we discovered that we had
to walk at least 25 km before we reached anywhere that had
accommodation. The air was clear and crisp, the countryside

breathtakingly beautiful, and we could see the route winding over the hills in front of us like a medieval map of the route to Jerusalem. Yet I took none of this in: all my energies were focused on worrying about the route ahead and the likelihood of finding somewhere to stay. As time went on I started imagining scenarios; I convinced myself that even if we found a hostel, it would probably be full and we would have to walk even further…

When we had reached the village, found the hostel, cooked a meal and were finally relaxing, my son turned to me and said, 'What a fabulous walk it was today.' I realized that in my desperate and ultimately purposeless worrying, I had missed all the treasures the day had to offer, and which I would never see again.

Besides major crises to overcome such as shipwrecks, attacks from brigands and encounters with the plague, early pilgrims had plenty of minor things to worry about as well. Although in some areas food would be plentiful, in others there was a distinct shortage. This might be due to crop failure, poor agricultural land or simply a lack of population to cultivate the soil. Several guidebooks of the time of the early pilgrims mention areas that are particularly sparse in food and drink, without offering much in a way of a solution to this problem.

In addition to worrying about accommodation and supplies, one's journey companions could also provide cause for concern. There are instances recorded of people joining pilgrim parties with the purpose of robbing genuine pilgrims, leaving them in a foreign country with no means of support or of returning home. Many pilgrims slept uneasily for the first few days of their journey, concern about their companions keeping them awake.

Although the contemporary pilgrim has much better access to supplies and accommodation than their forerunners, there is still much that can concern the modern-day traveller. Water supplies are a constant worry – especially if the weather is hot – and much is written on walkers' websites about the amount of water necessary to carry to avoid running out. This obviously varies according to the type of countryside you are walking through, but worrying about adequate water and food can take up a lot of time and energy.

On busy routes during the popular times of year for travelling, accommodation too can be in short supply. To arrive tired and exhausted at a hostel only to be told that it is full and that the next one is a matter of some kilometres away can turn what was a pleasant if somewhat hard-going day into one that pushes the limits of endurance. Unsurprisingly, accommodation worries are among those that trouble potential pilgrims the most.

To worry constantly is to allow the routine of the day to distract you from the joys of the journey. Far better to conserve one's energy, in order to deal better with a situation should it occur, than to waste it worrying over what might be!

Reflection

Before you begin the day's journey, take a handful of mud or earth. Rub it between your hands, allowing

it to run through your fingers as you let the earth
represent all the things that are worrying you about
the day ahead. Watch as your hands gradually get
dirtier, soiled by the small concerns of the day to
come. Your hands will become unfit to use – to eat
or drink with, to care for other people with – they
are so clogged with the dirt of worry. Now find some
clean running water to wash your hands. As you do
so, allow your worries to be washed out of your mind:
your hands and heart are now better prepared for
the journey ahead.

The Obstacle of Pain

Out of suffering have emerged the strongest
souls; the most massive characters are seared
with scars.

Khalil Gibran

The young man limped into the hostel. It was getting late: we had all showered and eaten and were writing our journals or studying maps and guides. To our surprise, the man did not take off his pack before going upstairs to find his bunk – he still had it on as he came down with his towel, heading for the bathroom. He hesitated in the doorway and then looked at me. Sitting there with my teenage son, clearly my face showed both age and sympathy! 'Do you mind?' he said. 'I've hurt my back. The straps have rubbed… I could do with some advice.' I got up and went with him into the bathroom. When he took off his pack, I could see from the blood that had soaked through his T-shirt that his back was in a bad way. Gingerly he peeled off his T-shirt, wincing as he did so. His back sported two large blisters, now rubbed raw, where the pack straps had been. Shocked into silence, I helped him clean up his back and try to fix some sort of padding to protect his wounds, sticking them up with plasters that were clearly inadequate for the job. He took painkillers, then limped upstairs to his bed, too tired to eat more than a sandwich.

The next day, having purchased more supplies from the pharmacy, we left the man resting in the hostel. He would be there for some time, but was determined to continue his journey. 'Worst case scenario,' he said bravely, 'I use carrier bags!'

Travelling conditions for pilgrims in the eleventh and twelfth centuries could be truly awful. Poor sanitation made personal hygiene extremely difficult. The food that could be obtained might not be of the best standard either. Aboard ship, a quantity of worms came with the meat as standard, as did the necessity of drinking putrid water and coping with the inevitable consequences. Once on dry land food might not be much better – one guide of the twelfth century stated that 'all fish, beef and pork in Spain and Galicia made foreigners ill'. To this was added all the local viruses and infections against which travellers lacked immunity, leaving pilgrims in a physically uncomfortable, if not life-threatening, condition. Extremes of weather also brought on suffering, with poor pilgrims being inadequately equipped either for great heat or severe cold.

Today we are less likely to suffer from major illnesses, but the day-to-day discomforts of living on the move will probably not leave you unaffected. If not suffering from the effects of bad food, you may well notice the difference that a change of diet makes to your wellbeing. This is not just because the food you are used to is not available locally, but the type of food you need to eat – high carbohydrate and lightweight if you are travelling – may be radically different to your normal diet.

Your clothing may also take getting used to. The discipline of wearing a hat if it is sunny and of protecting yourself from insects and adverse weather conditions both hot and cold may take some adjusting. However well-worn in you consider your boots to be, feet and footwear are a constant preoccupation!

Your pain may not be physical. Time spent alone may bring to the front of your mind many thoughts and memories that you would rather not dwell on and many feelings that you would rather not face (see Solitude, page 66).

A lot of effort can be misplaced trying to avoid pain, even of the mildest type. For this sort of journey, pain should be accepted as part of the process of transformation – not only is it inevitable, it is necessary if you are to grow and to change. Addressing fears, worries and pain, learning to deal with them – either by putting them aside and not allowing them to drain you of energy, or by facing them and living through them – is part of the route to understanding yourself and those with whom you share your world.

As you face each obstacle you can be sure that your steps will become steadier and your heart stronger. As Khalil Gibran writes: 'Your pain is the breaking of the shell that encloses your understanding.'

Reflection

Go out onto the pathway and find a stone about the size of your heart (the size of your clenched fist). Find one that appeals to you, that interests you or that you find attractive. Hold this stone and warm it in your hands. Examine it closely: look at its shape, its dents, its rough edges and the places where it has been worn smooth. Think of all the factors that have contributed to making this stone what it is – the type of stone, the weather, its location. This stone is unique: all the things that have happened to it have shaped it and made it the way it is. Reflect on your own heart, the pain and sorrow that you hold within it. Think about how these have shaped you and made you the unique being that you are. Think of sorrows that have made you stronger, and those that have weakened or damaged you. As you hold the stone, be grateful for all of these. Put your stone down carefully, by a tree or a bush, by something beautiful or interesting. Prepare to face whatever pain your life might bring you in the future, allowing it to strengthen your heart and increase your understanding of the world.

Rest and Restoration

Sacred Places on the Way

People need a sacred narrative. They must have a sense of larger purpose, in one form or another, however intellectualized. They will find a way to keep ancestral spirits alive.

E. O. Wilson, from *The Biological Basis of Morality*

It was one of the first pilgrimages we had undertaken as a family, and we were still learning how to pace ourselves and what to expect from the journey. The previous day it had rained almost non-stop; walking had been an effort and conversation was minimal as each member of the group concentrated on not losing their footing on the muddy footpath. Today, however, the sun shone brightly and our spirits were lifted fractionally as we began the day's walk, slightly uncomfortable in our still damp clothes.

As the day wore on, the sun burned hotter. From longing for an end to the rain yesterday, we hoped it might start again. The track rose up higher into the hills and there was no sign of habitation for miles, just rolling scrubland, gradually becoming wilder and more barren as we climbed. Then, as we rounded a bend in the track, we came across a small patch of the greenest grass, edged with trees. In the centre stood a stone shrine, no bigger than a garden shed, marked with a cross. We tried the door. It was open, and we crept into its cool darkness. As our eyes grew accustomed to the light we saw a statue of Mary at one end with a few wooden chairs facing it. We sat in the quiet stillness, letting the peace of the place sink into our bodies and spirits. Even the baby was quiet, sensitive perhaps to the atmosphere of veneration and prayer. We gave thanks.

The medieval respect for saints was a product of the age. Imagine a world in which every part of your life – your job, where you will live, the sort of person you will be allowed to marry – is rigidly set: you are within a fixed class structure, and your options in life are extremely limited. In contrast to your social world is the natural one, in which all is allowed to proceed unchecked – you are at the mercy of strange phenomena, powerful storms, failing harvests, mysterious illnesses.

If there is no explanation for these occurrences in this world, you must look to the next to find a reason and purpose. The veneration of saints was an expression of the belief that forces from beyond this world had an influence on the events that surrounded the medieval citizen. Saints – holy people who in their lives on earth had accomplished extraordinary wonders – had the power to influence these supernatural phenomena, for good or bad. By praying to these saints pilgrims could persuade them to alter things in the pleader's favour. But there is more: the objects that the saints left behind in this world – clothing, things they used and, particularly, their body parts – were still imbued with the residue of holiness that made them so powerful in heaven. It was believed that this residual power could be acquired if a person were to touch these objects, or, by extension, to visit the places that were familiar to the saint, and pray at the altar of the church where their bodies were buried. Tales of miracles that occurred in these chapels and churches served to reinforce the belief that God wanted those relics venerated, and the saints did work to the benefit of those who made the pilgrimage to their birthplace or burial site.

There was, of course, a strict hierarchy of saints, with some, such as St Peter, being extremely powerful and others having little power outside the particular branch of healing with which they were associated (see Healing, page 81). The type of pilgrimage made to these holy places also varied depending on the importance of the request. Thanksgiving for a life saved might necessitate a trip to Santiago; lost keys would perhaps only merit a prayer in the nearest church dedicated to St Jude. Similarly, the chapels, churches and shrines that were associated with the life of each saint had varying degrees of prestige and fame. A church that possessed the finger of St Peter, for example, might still be accorded more honour than one that possessed the entire body of a lesser saint. Very popular saints, such as Thomas à Becket, might find themselves venerated anywhere that a connection could be found: there is a cross at Newington in honour of the fact that St Thomas had confirmed local schoolchildren on that site. The greater the association and the more powerful the saint, the more popular the church. This was important, since the more visitors a church entertained, the more offerings were made to that institution. Increased riches led to increased power, more imposing buildings and a spiral of success.

On a lengthy pilgrimage, such as to Rome or Santiago, the way would be dotted with chapels, churches and shrines, dedicated to local and world-famous saints, each requiring the pilgrim to stop and pray there – for themselves and for the success and safety of their journey. This continuous process of prayer would stand them in good stead when the Day of Judgment came.

The contemporary pilgrim might be tempted to make light of these minor pilgrim places, viewing them as distractions away from the main task, the final destination. However, even if we might feel the twinges of scepticism as we read of yet another astoundingly holy life and visit the place where so many miraculous healings and happenings are claimed to have taken place, there is a role for these places in our journey. They can offer a chance for rest and reflection, an opportunity to reset our spiritual goals for the journey, and to assess how far we have travelled, in mind as well as in body. These places can give us an insight into the character of the region through which we are travelling – the saints that are honoured often embody the values of a community. Small pilgrim places can be truly sacred spaces, witnesses to centuries of fervent prayer, containers for the hopes and dreams of thousands of ordinary people who followed the same route in their time as we do in ours. They can remind us that we are part of that great 'cloud of witnesses', both seen and unseen, who have gone before us and will follow after us – a moment of connection with all humanity.

Reflection

Buy a postcard of the church you have just visited. Cut or tear it into jigsaw pieces. Scatter these pieces in front of you and look at them, meaningless and powerless. Take one piece and think about yourself – how far you have journeyed, how far you have yet to go. Think about your relationship with other people – consider whether it is fragmented and scattered or unifying and whole. Gradually assemble the pieces, thinking about the people to whom you are most closely connected. Think about those who make you whole, who interact with you and complement your existence. As you build the jigsaw, consider those people who are less important to you but who nevertheless play a vital part in making the picture complete. Pause before you fit the last piece in the puzzle – think of the people who are no longer on this earth, whose going has left a gap in your life. As you fit the final piece into place, remember that we are all part of the same creation.

Labyrinth

The Sacred Path

Walking the labyrinth invites us back to the centre of our being.

Lauren Artress, from *Walking a Sacred Path*

It was New Year's Eve, and my family and I were in Amiens, in northern France. I had been reading a lot about labyrinths – complex designs consisting of a single path which winds its way circuitously to the centre of the pattern. They were used as a means of prayer, but I did not understand how walking a twisting pathway could possibly help anyone to pray. I had read Lauren Artress' book, *Walking a Sacred Path*, and though sceptical of her many claims for the powers of the labyrinth, I was determined to try to walk it.

The most famous Christian labyrinth is in Chartres Cathedral, and it was there that we had gone originally. But the beautiful, mysterious pattern laid into the stone floor had been covered by hundreds of chairs, and every time we went near them we were shepherded away. So we were in Amiens, whose labyrinth was uncovered. And in the dim light of a freezing cold cathedral we walked the labyrinth.

It was a curiously moving experience – six people following the twists and turns of a complex pattern laid out on the ground. We were contained by the pattern and yet free to move at our own pace within it. We were in a community of walkers, yet separate from one another, following the same path to the same destination but each at their own pace. As with the pace, so the insights gained were individual, unique to each walker.

The first thing any labyrinth walker learns is that to look ahead, to try to trace out the development of the pattern while walking, is to invite disaster. I have always been well organized – on occasion to the point of obsession. The further ahead I can plan, the more secure I feel. But when I tried to spy out my way through the twists and turns of the labyrinth, I moved off the path, looking down at my feet again only to discover that I was retracing my steps back to the beginning instead of moving forward. Seeing the labyrinth as a metaphor for life, I learnt that sometimes we must be content to follow the path that is set before us, putting one foot in front of another in an act of faith that the centre will be arrived at, eventually.

As the popularity of pilgrimage waxed and waned, another sort of journey was developing. Parallel to the decline in numbers undertaking physical pilgrimage, it is possible to chart a slight rise in the notion of the inner journey, the spiritual pilgrimage. Fortified by the teachings of St Augustine, and St Gregory of Nyssa's affirmation that change of place does not necessarily bring one closer to God, and St Jerome's concern about 'the neglecting of everyday duties in favour of pilgrimage to the Holy Land', methods were sought that would result in the same sense of journeying as physical travel without having to leave one's community. The answer seemed to be the labyrinth.

Labyrinths are thousands of years old. Although it was Herodotus who first coined the name in 484 BC, labyrinths had existed well before then – there is archaeological evidence of an Egyptian labyrinth in 1000 BC. Their materials vary from stone, outlines in stone, tiles (Roman) to turf (in Britain), although they all share the vital feature of a labyrinth having only one path leading to the centre and the same path out.

During the twelfth century the actions of the Crusades made travel difficult and dangerous. Therefore, seven churches in Europe were appointed as pilgrimage churches – churches to which a pilgrimage would be the same as a trip to Jerusalem. Gradually the idea of a substitute for pilgrimage was gaining ground. Then, in the time between 1194 and 1220, the great labyrinth of Chartres Cathedral was built. Forty-two feet in diameter with a path sixteen feet wide, the labyrinth is full of symbolism. The path is 861½ feet long – the number of days' journey to Jerusalem and back – and at the centre is a six-petal rose representing the six days of creation and the rose of St Mary the Virgin. If it were placed flat, the centre of the great rose window at the west end of the cathedral would match the central rose of the labyrinth.

No one is sure how labyrinths were used – perhaps as a way of ending a pilgrimage, since the central rose design was also called Jerusalem. Perhaps they were walked as preparation for church services, as a way of calming the spirit, but however they were used, the worn stones testify to thousands of feet walking the complex pattern over the centuries. With the rationalism of the Renaissance, labyrinth-walking lost popularity, and many of the cathedral labyrinths were destroyed, with Chartres housing the only original floor labyrinth.

Walking the labyrinth is a mystical experience, as Artress writes: 'It has been assigned properties of healing – mental, physical and spiritual, given the role of helping through its own complexity to untangle the inner soul to find peace. It has been used as a metaphor for life's journey, with attempts to look ahead and spy out the twists and turns of the paths leading to confusion, its apparent doubling back and veering away the representation of the unexpected events that overtake our lives.' It is used to gain clarity of mind when seeking to solve problems and as a way of prayer. For the contemporary pilgrim, a labyrinth can be used in many ways. It can be used as preparation for the pilgrimage itself, the path of the labyrinth symbolizing the path of self-discovery that is the pilgrim's inner route as well as the lengthy journeying that is the outer. It can be used during the journey and at the destination as a way of celebrating the pathway and one's place on it. It can also be used as a pilgrimage in itself – just as the pilgrims used Chartres as a substitute for Jerusalem, so those unable to travel great distances physically can use the mental journey of the labyrinth.

Reflection

Trace the outline of a labyrinth in the ground with your finger (see Appendix, page 127). Follow its path, and reflect on where you are on the path of your pilgrimage and on the path of your life's journey. Place a stone on the labyrinth on the point where you think you are right now, and give thanks. If you have enough space, trace a labyrinth large enough to walk. Use your experience of walking the labyrinth as a metaphor for your journey so far. Stop and reflect at the places that draw you to do so. When you arrive in the centre, pause again for as long as you wish, then follow the same path out.

The Journey's End and the Return Home

Arrival

**You are not here to verify
instruct yourself or inform curiosity
or carry report. You are here to kneel
where prayer has been valid.**

T. S. Eliot, from *The Four Quartets*

After weeks of journeying, of getting used to the deprivations
and hardships of the journey and promising myself endless small
luxuries when I finally arrive at my destination (nice coffee, hot
bath, no snoring within 100 miles of my bed), getting to the end
of a pilgrimage is a strange and somewhat painful experience.
If the pilgrimage site is a major one, such as Rome or Santiago,
the last miles of the journey will take place in rather unpleasant
surroundings – paths often wind through endless suburbs,
difficult to navigate and uncomfortable to walk. Gradually,
the clothes that have served you so well and have been so

appropriate in the wilds of the countryside seem more and more
unkempt and unsuitable. The first glimpse of the destination
is usually from some distance, and appears to remain at that
distance for far too long. Finally, long after I thought I would get
there I emerge, usually from round the side of the building, and
stagger to the main door, pausing for a while in the square at the
front, aware that the goal of my wanderings has been reached.
And it always feels like an anticlimax. Entering the dimly lit
cathedral, pausing to say a prayer and light a candle, alone yet
invariably surrounded by many other people, I feel a sense of
detachment. Although five minutes before I was certain that I
could not walk another step, suddenly I want to be back on the
road again. And there and then are planted the seeds for the
next pilgrimage.

Throughout time, pilgrimage sites have been noisy and
distracting. When at last weary pilgrims found the way
to their destination, having survived the dangers and
deprivations of the journey, they would find the square
in front of the church or cathedral just as full as we
do today. The place would be full of stallholders, each
competing with the other to recommend their wares
to the jaded traveller. Fresh food and water would be
available along with a wide choice of souvenirs. Made
of clay or pewter, ceramic or stone, these would provide
proof for those at home that the destination was actually
reached, the entire journey really completed. Each site
had its own symbol: St Peter and St Paul for Rome; the
palm of Jericho for Jerusalem; and, the most famous

of all symbols, the shell for Santiago de Compostela. Designed to remind pilgrims that the coffin of St James had washed up on that coast centuries after his death and burial covered with scallop shells, and later transported to Santiago for veneration, this emblem, as mentioned previously, has become the universal sign for all pilgrims and not just those on the Camino de Santiago. The triumphant pilgrim would proudly purchase a scallop shell and place it in his hat as a sign of his success – and his increased holiness. For arriving at the site was more than just reaching the end of the journey: it entailed completing the task that had originally been embarked upon – that of seeking forgiveness, blessing, healing; that of fulfilling a vow, honouring an oath; that of kneeling finally before the tomb of the saint who could bring what the pilgrim had sought.

For the modern pilgrim, this last importance, attached so firmly to the destination for the medieval pilgrim, may be missing. After all, the purpose of pilgrimage today is perhaps not to arrive, but to journey well; not to solve things, but to make us more aware of them. It is at least as much about travelling hopefully as it is about arriving. So the end of your journey may be tinged with anticlimax. You may feel adrift: after so many days of journeying with a purpose, finally reaching your destination can leave you feeling empty. But true pilgrimage does not end abruptly in time or place; it is a continuous state. It may not be the destination that transforms, but the process of travelling, of being one more person to have journeyed a route that allows us to explore the geography of our own hearts. We journey to find the sacred and the holy, and we find ourselves, for that is what we all are.

Return

We shall not cease from our exploration
And the end of all our exploring
Will be to arrive where we started
And know the place for the first time.
T. S. Eliot, from *The Four Quartets*

There was a small group of young people waiting at the station. I had noticed them at intervals on the route – we had even walked together for one day's journey, but they had stopped at different places, preferring to rest in the larger towns with more nightlife, while I had spent my rest days in small villages or settlements. They had been one of the joys of the journey, full of life and energy, always cheerful even on the most dismal parts of the route. They had not known each other before this pilgrimage but had come together on the very first day, seeking each other out because of their youth, standing out among the many grey hairs of the average pilgrim. Drawn from different places and different countries, they had been through an intense experience together, and now they were going home. For the first time since I had met them, they were not cheerful. Tears were pouring down the faces of the girls, and the guys looked at the ground and scuffed their boots. One of the girls turned to me: 'I can't bear it,' she cried. 'We have been through so much together and changed so much and now we have to go. And I feel so different and my family will just see the same old me, and only these people know how it feels. And there were days and days when I just wanted the journey to end and now it has and part of my heart has died.'

We have observed already that many pilgrims never arrived back home. The dangers of the journey – pestilence, wild animals and bandits – meant that considerably fewer pilgrims finally opened the doors of their homes after their travels than had originally set out upon them. And the perils of the journey were of course doubled by the fact that, having arrived at the shrine, prayed and given offerings, the pilgrim then had to turn about and make the same long and dangerous journey home. Not many pilgrims could afford the cost of a sea journey from a site back to England, and that form of transport could in any case be just as dangerous as travelling overland. It is not surprising that many pilgrims, particularly those to the furthest and most inaccessible site of Jerusalem, chose instead to spend the rest of their lives there and not to return home at all!

For those who did, the return journey must have seemed lengthy and draining. With their duty of prayer done, the satisfaction of a completed pilgrimage must have seemed a high price to pay as the pilgrim retraced his steps along the path. Years might have passed, certainly months, and much might have changed at home. Even more depressing, nothing might have changed, and a pilgrim who had travelled so far and experienced so much that was new and interesting might find picking up the familiar routine a very difficult task. For such reasons and more, many pilgrims would make more than one pilgrimage, sometimes even visiting the same sites again!

For the pilgrim today, the return can be just as difficult. Modern communication means that family and friends will have some idea of the time of your arrival. Modern travel means that they will have some idea of the places you have been and the things you have seen. But a journey such as a pilgrimage, packed with incident and experience, used for reflection and growth, can change people deeply, and to those expecting the same person to return as who went, these changes can be quite a shock. This can make your arrival a very bittersweet experience – you want to communicate all that has happened to you but don't know quite where to start. You might feel a completely different person, but this changed character can be difficult to define or explain. How are you going to fit your new self into your old environment without upsetting those around you or losing the precious gifts of self-awareness and transformation given to you on the pilgrimage? Many people who have made a particular pilgrimage together make great efforts to stay in touch, in order to make sense of and retain something of that inner journey and transformation.

The key to reintegration is to take it slowly. On your arrival home take time to be still. Resist the urge to hurl yourself into the midst of where you left off. Take time to unpack mentally as well as physically. Wait a few days before you begin to tell everyone about your travels, giving your spirit time to absorb all that has happened and to make sense of it within the context of your everyday life. After all, the real journey is the one that begins when you start living your transformation. We go, only to return and begin again.

Reflection
In your journal describe in as much detail as possible a souvenir from your journey, how you acquired it, and why it means so much to you.

Reflection
Draw a picture of one of the doors you saw on your travels – it does not have to be completely accurate as long as you know which door it is and where you saw it. Use this door as a metaphor for the threshold of your new life post-pilgrimage. Picture the two scenes that are bounded by the door – the scene that makes up your life pre-pilgrimage, and the landscape or situation that you are moving towards now. How are they different?

Appendix:
Drawing a Labyrinth

1. Begin with a simple outline of a cross, drawn into the ground or on a piece of paper: with four dots as shown.
2. Connect the top arm of the central cross to the dot on the right.
3. Connect the top left dot to the right arm of the cross.

3. Move across the cross to the left, then draw outside the loop to meet the bottom right dot, moving in a clockwise direction.
4. Continue until all the lines and dots are connected as shown.